Supernatural
Healing
Today

Supernatural Healing Today

by

Trevor Dearing, M.A., B.D.

Logos International
Plainfield, New Jersey

Unless otherwise noted as KJV (King James
Version), all Scripture passages are taken
from the Revised Standard Version of the
Bible (RSV).

SUPERNATURAL HEALING TODAY
Copyright ©1979 by Logos International
All rights reserved
Printed in the United States of America
Library of Congress Catalog Card Number: 78-71527
International Standard Book Number: 0-88270-324-2
Logos International, Plainfield, New Jersey 07060

To Anne, my wife and closest
companion in this healing
adventure, with love.

Acknowledgments

Once again I wish to thank my gallant band of helpers—typists Winifred Chapman, Enid Holt, and members of the Pinhoe Christian Fellowship, Exeter; script reviewer, Jim Rattenbury, and the editors of Logos International—for all their hard work. I am so actively engaged in the work of divine healing that, without such help, I would never have had time to write about it! I want to express gratitude to my bishop, John Trillo of Chelmsford, who has stood as firm as a rock behind me and encouraged me to allow my ministry to develop and reach out to the farthest corners of the earth. He has commended my work to bishops, clergy, and ministers all over the world. I wish also to express sincere thanks to the thirty members of the Power, Praise and Healing Mission team, who shared deeply in my healing mission in the two years following my leaving the church of St. Paul, Hainault. They gave themselves unstintingly to the Lord and to me and were a source of fellowship, strength, encouragement, and inspiration during a difficult transition period to an itinerant ministry.

Contents

PART ONE

SUPERNATURALISM TODAY

1

Hitting the Headlines

"Miracle Hands Have Healed Me," "Many Find New Hope and Happiness at Healing Services," "They Came from Miles Around to be Healed," "Hundreds Queue as Faith Healer, Trevor, Hits the Town," "Drama as Deaf Woman Claims Miracle Cure," "Healer Packs 'Em in Like a Pop Star," "Churches Filled to Capacity for Power, Praise and Healing."

Headlines like these have appeared in newspapers all over England since I left St. Paul's, Hainault, in November 1975 and set out on a traveling healing ministry. Even before that, however, events had been remarkable enough, as thousands of sick people had flocked to my small, East London, parish church, in search of supernatural healing. Local residents had been amazed as crowds, including people from as far away as Paris, Austria, the U.S.A., Canada, and even Singapore, had gathered outside the building many hours before healing services were due to begin. These people had not only read about my healing ministry in local newspapers, but also seen documentaries in magazines, from the traditional *Woman* to the trendy *Street Life*.

Services at the church had also been given unsolicited, nationwide television coverage at peak viewing times. These programs featured many claims to healing. A Southend doctor who had been suffering from chronic depression, and women afflicted with such conditions as acute colitis, depression, and heroin addiction, told the stories of their deliverances. A multiple sclerosis patient also declared that his life had been revolutionized by attending meetings at the church.

Eventually, the news reached other European countries by way of "Eurovision." This led to reporters from Holland and Belgium writing extensive articles about my ministry. Interest was even aroused in Canada and I was interviewed for a feature program in that country. The American *National Courier* also carried an account of some healings which had been verified by the medical profession. This was entitled "Doctors and Cured Patients Acclaim the Amazing Healing Powers of the Mod Minister."

This publicity forced me into a crisis situation as I became increasingly flooded with requests to take services at other churches, many of which were far away from Hainault. It seemed that God might well be calling us to leave the church where we were so happy and where so much was still happening, to take this message and ministry all over England and, indeed, the world.

Eventually I met with my bishop to discuss the implications of my developing ministry. The requests for missions were pouring in and everywhere I went blessings abounded. I felt in my spirit a growing calling to a ministry of dynamic evangelism and a diminishing of my feeling for pastoral care and oversight. My wife, Anne, had the same witness. We needed, however, real evidence from outside ourselves.

The bishop had informed us that in an itinerant ministry I could neither be housed nor financed by the diocese, and both were essential for a family of six. It was obvious that the Lord would have to undertake and that such provision would be an evidence of His leading. Almost at once two Christian men, both wonderfully alive in the Spirit, without any approach from myself, offered to buy a house in order to provide accommodation for my family. The house which we felt would be ideal turned out to be priced at exactly the amount of money which could be raised for the venture.

A trust was formed and soon trustees and a team of helpers were ready for action under the banner: "Power, Praise, and Healing Mission." Money seemed to come from the most unexpected sources to provide for our needs. Our first outreach meetings were more blessed than ever. The Lord was indicating the new direction my ministry had to take.

After discussion about keeping the archbishop's "Guidelines on Exorcism" which would be necessary for me to retain my place as a minister in the Church of England, I received my bishop's blessing and promise of support for the exciting new adventure of faith.

The news flashed across the nation. The massive circulation *Daily Mirror* headlined it as "Vicar is Free-lance Exorcist." The *Daily Mail* declared "Exorcist Vicar Takes to the Road," and the *Times:* "Vicar Resigns to Devote Himself to Exorcism."

In the *Times*, Clifford Langley, the religious affairs correspondent, wrote:

> The Rev. Trevor Dearing, one of the leading practitioners of exorcism in the Church of England, has tendered his resignation as Vicar of St. Paul's, Hainault, in Essex. He said yesterday that he wanted to be free of parish duties so that he could devote his whole time to exorcism, faith healing, and prayer meetings. . . . Mr. Dearing said he had the full support of the Bishop of Chelmsford, the Right Rev. John Trillo, in continuing his work on an itinerant basis.

Religious journals like the *Church Times* and *Church of England Newspaper* debated the rightness of this move and I was asked to appear on television to discuss the issues involved.

However, late in 1975 we became well and truly launched. Journalists from national newspapers and periodicals asked if they could accompany me on some of my journeys and later wrote prominent articles about my ministry. National television also continued to be interested in all that was taking place in my traveling healing ministry.

This was no seven-day wonder. It was not a temporary filling in of a news vacuum. The interest continued on a vast scale, well beyond the confines of the church. It was apparent that supernatural healing was a matter of wide public, as well as ecclesiastical, interest in the 1970s.

This was also shown when one day the telephone rang just as I was climbing into my car to go away for my summer vacation. Reluctantly, I went back to the house to take this last-minute call.

"This is Wendy Jones of Midland's Television," said a sweet, very feminine voice. "Will you appear on my program, 'Platform for Today, Ladies' Night'?"

I said that I would and this led to my appearing on a program to demonstrate and debate the whole matter of exorcism and divine healing.

It was a rather fearsome, nerve-shattering ordeal, because not only was the medical profession represented by a skeptical woman doctor, but also the National Secular Society was there to have their say. It soon became apparent that outspoken critics and opponents were well-represented in the all-woman studio audience. The debate went to and fro, until the program was drawing to a close.

"We have three ladies here who would like you to lay hands on them," explained an excited Wendy. Cheerfully, she went on, "Will you minister to them and we shall investigate their progress and let the viewers know just what has happened."

I shot an arrow prayer to heaven. "Jesus, Lord!" I exclaimed, "now we're in a spot. You can't be seen, but together we are on television. I can't heal them, but you can. Lord, I trust you as I act for your glory."

This was *really* twentieth century divine healing!

I had made sure that the ladies were, in fact, very sincere and really believed that Jesus could heal them. It was not to be a gimmicky act, but a living reality. I asked the Christians in the studio to pray. I laid my hands on the first lady, who was suffering terribly from arthritis. As I prayed, she sank to the floor under the power of the Holy Spirit. Wendy Jones tried vainly to catch the next lady to whom I ministered healing, this time for severe pain due to a hiatal hernia. The third person, a woman with a severely ulcerated leg, eventually completed the pile of bodies on the floor.

A week later, in a special news feature, these ladies claimed either to have been completely healed or to be very much better.

The public, therefore, would not let the matter drop. So great was the demand for my ministry that thousands of letters and scores of telephone calls came to my home and the studios of I.T.V., Birmingham. Audience rating procedures showed that all past viewing records for the program had been broken. A second, and even third program were demanded, and thousands of people rushed to meetings I held especially for them in many parts of Britain.

As my own ministry of divine healing developed in this unprecedented and entirely unforseen way, I discovered, to my delight, that many other people and churches engaged in this ministry were experiencing something of the same response from the British public. Sometimes the publicity, as in my case, was sensational. In many instances, however, the ministry was proceeding regularly and quietly, but nevertheless with definite results. A revival of healing methods dating back nearly two thousand years to New Testament times was becoming a fact in more and more churches in our land.

Eventually, I began to be involved in similar manifestations of God's healing power in other parts of the world. In Singapore, the cathedral was packed to overflowing as, together with the bishop, my wife, and six clergy, I ministered to hundreds of people. The whole diocese received a divine visitation.

My ministry overseas was given a new impetus when Dan Malachuk, president of Logos International, heard what God was doing through my ministry in England and invited me to take the final meeting of the Third World Conference on the Holy Spirit at Jerusalem. As I stood before that huge gathering of people from many nations, I felt inadequate, yet thrilled. God graciously poured out His Holy Spirit upon us as I ministered to the needs of hundreds of people until past midnight.

This conference led to an invitation to minister in Finland, where, as in England, crowds packed into the churches. As my wife and I laid hands on people the blessing saturated them, and there were moving scenes as many desperate needs were met by God.

In 1977, at the next world conference, in Switzerland, we ministered to over a thousand people from forty-three different nations. This led to many more invitations to minister abroad.

I began to read many books about divine healing and discovered that this new moving of the Spirit of God in supernatural power, in which I had become involved, seemed to have begun in America with the early Pentecostals. Then Oral Roberts, T.L. Osborn, and Kathryn Kuhlman became important movers in this realm as crowds of many thousands gathered at their healing meetings. I found it thrilling to realize, however, that God was now using ordinary Anglican parsons like myself as "channels of blessing" in what was definitely a vast resurgence of divine, miraculous, supernatural healing in the middle of the twentieth century.

2

The Comeback
of the Supernatural

Over the years my evangelistic healing services have
developed their own particular form and ethos. They
emanate and breathe the supernatural presence and
power of God. Stuart Hyslop, a reporter from the
Southend *Evening Echo*, gave his impressions:

Everything is relaxed. Some people have been
before, many will be from different churches,
different religions—or have no religion at all.
There is no ritual, few trappings. Mr. Dearing,
apart from his clerical collar, dresses as casually as
most of the congregation. Music comes from a small
group and from the church organ. It is catchy,
unrestrained and all about joy and putting your trust
and love in Jesus. Everyone sings cheerfully—people
leap from their seats, waving their hands.
There are cries of "Hallelujah." Mr. Dearing walks
about the front of the church, sometimes he talks to
the congregation and joins in the singing. Then Mr.
Dearing and the congregation pray and he bursts out

speaking in "tongues." Immediately Mr. Dearing stops speaking, a member of the congregation bursts out with a fluent, flowing, English interpretation.

When Mr. Dearing makes his call for the sick to come forward, many respond, some in calipers and on crutches and in wheelchairs. Throughout the meeting there is a sense of expectancy. There is always the possibility that someone may have a miracle cure as has happened so often before, or that Mr. Dearing may have to struggle with a demon.

Ian Mather of the *Observer* was present with me at meetings held in Northern Ireland. He wrote:

One meeting in a suite at Belfast's Europa Hotel ended up with people lying all over the carpet in a state of ecstasy after Mr. Dearing had laid hands on them.

As the service continued the atmosphere became even more emotional. Mr. Dearing, now jacketless in clerical collar, his eyes half-closed, demanded diseases to depart. Above the sound of gentle hymn singing he could be heard shouting commands. "Arthritis, I banish you from every joint and bone." "Eye! Receiving healing." "All nasal passages be free in Jesus' name."

People keeled over backwards and soon bodies littered the floor. In front of me two women lay next to each other. Later they came round, they held each other's hands, laughing and crying at the same time.

The Comeback of the Supernatural

This falling—"being slain by the Spirit" as some call it—has biblical precedents (2 Chron. 5:14, Mark 9:26, Acts 9:4, Rev. 1:17). It is a feature of powerful ministry and certainly heightens the sense of the supernatural. One can actually *see* that God is moving in people's lives. The recipients can also feel and sense that the Spirit of God has come upon them in blessing. From the beginning to the end of such meetings I have been consciously "anointed" and "immersed" in the Spirit, moving and acting for hours at a time in the realm of the supernatural.

After the emotions of joy, wonder, love, and even awe, have diminished and I have come down to earth again, I have often reflected upon the ironies and contradictions of it all.

"Whatever have I been doing?" I have asked myself. "Am I really sane? Have I been dreaming?"

Had this been happening in some rather primitive, uneducated, half-civilized society, I could more easily have understood it. Perhaps the people would have been too ignorant to know what was impossible. But here I was, an academic man, a graduate of two universities, holder of a high honors degree, ministering what could be regarded as "mumbo jumbo" in twentieth century, Western, cultured nations!

Basically, I always acknowledged myself to be a child of the rationalistic age in which I lived. My five years of intense theological training had included papers in philosophy, comparative religions, and psychology. My course had proved to be so intellectual, liberal, and entirely credible that the whole of the Bible appeared to need drastic reinterpretation in order to make any sense to people living today. Thus I gained my degrees and, in the process, I lost my Bible!

I had, therefore, been schooled in the thought-forms of man-come-of-age, who shouted, "Glory to Man in the highest! for Man is the master of things!" I was one of a generation who felt we had at last succeeded in getting this universe nicely "buttoned up." We now understood the scientific laws by which it had always worked. Nature could be relied upon to behave itself in very predictable ways, and, to prove it, we had sent men on journeys to and from the moon.

Like all my contemporaries, I was conscious that I lived in a world of nuclear reactors, supersonic aircraft, global television, skyscrapers, and, not least, massive developments in medical science. X-rays, the microscope, and advances in the field of biochemistry had vastly increased our ability to diagnose and treat physical maladies. True, such serious illnesses as cancer, muscular dystrophy and multiple sclerosis still baffled the experts. On the grounds of past success, however, there was hope that these, and other incurable sicknesses, would one day be conquered, until only old age would be terminal.

All forms of emotional and personality disorders, neuroses and psychoses, were now also having the lid taken off them, and the terrible distress caused by them was being much alleviated by drugs and psychotherapy.

In a world such as this, the area of the miraculous had been rapidly narrowing as gaps in human knowledge, previously filled by God, had diminished. It was, therefore, very logical that pastors like myself should be taught how to bury the dead, but not how to heal the sick.

The Comeback of the Supernatural

As for exorcisms, we had been told that the demons of the New Testament were to be consigned to the garbage cans of first-century superstition.

The enemies of supernaturalism still abound within the church as well as outside it. In the last decade American theologians have declared that God is dead, in other words, for all practical purposes, He just doesn't exist. I had once believed this to be a true reflection of the religious thought of our time.

Yet, as I surveyed my own new, international, miracle ministry, I began to become more and more confident that a supernatural revolution was taking place. Results themselves also showed that I was really onto something real, revolutionary, and tremendously exciting. So much that I heard and read from all over the world confirmed that I wasn't just an oddity or a crank. It was undeniable. The supernatural was making a comeback.

This is indeed a fact of today! Evidence of increasing supernatural phenomena mounts up daily from many parts of the world. Twentieth-century people, from all educational backgrounds and walks of life, are claiming to speak in heavenly languages, to utter oracles direct from God, to see visions, to predict events leading to the end of the world and to be inspired by the Holy Spirit with wisdom and knowledge beyond all natural possibilities. They are actually exorcising evil spirits and communicating supernatural healing. The events of the New Testament which rationalists have written off are being reenacted in a scientific and technological age!

The truth is that man is instinctively, naturally, and inevitably religious and that the spiritual realm can no more tolerate a vacuum than can the natural. The winds of supernaturalism *are*, therefore, blowing at gale force, and they can refill the human spirit either with the breath of God or more sinister, damaging, and deadly counterfeits. They can either blow the ship of human history home to its destiny or smash humanity on the rocks of occultism and superstition. In days when films about supernaturalism fill our movie theaters, and when British newspapers report that most Americans believe in the supernatural, this phenomenon, a fact of our age, cannot and must not be ignored. Hope or disillusionment, final success or abysmal failure, faith or fear, life or death, heaven or hell, depend upon our understanding what is happening and using this God-given, spiritual power for the well-being of mankind. This is especially true of the ministry of healing which, among all the supernatural phenomena of our time, is the object of the greatest public interest and the source of much desperate hope.

3

An Important Distinction

I had not long been involved in ministering healing when I realized that a vital distinction had to be made. I discovered that not all supernatural healing is Christian. "Spiritual healing," "faith healing," and "divine healing" are not interchangeable descriptions of the same phenomenon. The term, "faith healing," puts all the emphasis on our "trust" in anything or anyone. It says nothing at all about God. Christian healing, however, is not merely about a psychological attitude which can produce good results. It affirms the necessity of an openness of spirit and soul to the God and Father of our Lord Jesus Christ.

"Spiritual healing" has even more confusing and dangerous overtones. It is the favorite expression of spiritualistic mediums who lay hands on sick people. They believe that some departed human beings now have spiritual power which they can channel to the sick through psychic men, women, and even children.

By contrast, the ministry of divine healing is based on the person and work of the Lord Jesus Christ. It begins with Him, continues in Him, and ends in Him. It is centered on Jesus of Nazareth, who went about healing all manner of sickness and disease among the people of first-century Palestine (Acts 10:38). Christians believe that this Jesus, now risen from the dead, is the "same yesterday and today and for ever" (Heb. 13:8). Divine healing, therefore, emanates from Jesus Christ. It results, not only in the well-being of suffering people, but also in glory and honor, praise and thanksgiving, being ascribed to Him by all who experience and witness His mighty works for mankind.

I experienced this divine healing myself when I was only nineteen years of age. At that time I was a mental, physical, and spiritual wreck.[1] I was not then a Christian, having been brought up in a typical, good, middle-class, but nonreligious, family. However, when I heard the gospel of the risen Jesus preached for the first time, I eagerly responded. I began to enter into a deep relationship with the Lord and the process of healing began.

Now, twenty-six years later, medical examinations have resulted only in reports of very good health. I have been able to marry a wonderful wife, to be a father of four lovely children, and to undertake a world-wide ministry of evangelism and healing. I have had no recurrence of my former illnesses. Jesus Christ has made me whole.

I was, without a doubt, healed through a deep relationship with Christ and can bear my own testimony to the power of a living God, who heals the sick.

This is divine healing. It is about God's healing power through His Son, our Savior Jesus Christ. It is, therefore,

---

[1] See my book *Supernatural Superpowers* (published by Logos International) for a full description of my terrible, hopeless condition.

in all its aspects, essentially Christian. It is this exclusive Christocentric emphasis which differentiates it from all other forms of supernatural healing.[2]

These other forms exist in most other world religions, and go back to animism, the religion of primitive, pagan man. Witch doctors have existed from time immemorial and have wielded great power through their definite abilities to make people either sick by cursing, or to make them well by "blessing." In the massive resurgence of supernaturalism today these practices have been reintroduced into our civilized society. They take the form of black magic if they are for cursing and white magic if they are for blessing. In England, covens of witches and warlocks are rapidly increasing and have attracted the attention of the media. In my ministry I am frequently meeting people who have become involved in these activities. Some have needed exorcism. The Bishop of Truro, Cornwall, recently showed me a collection of sinister charms which have come into his possession, handed over by people who have sought his help.

The most widespread revival of pagan healing, however, is in spiritism or, as its devotees prefer to call it, spiritualism. It is very prevalent in modern society, being a refined form of invoking spirits to the aid of men. The *Times* obituary of Mr. Harry Edwards, the best-known of psychic healers, who died last year, claimed that he made "spiritual healing" respectable. Apparently, he needed sixty secretaries to deal with his vast daily correspondence. He once wrote to me about people becoming well as "responding to spirit." Certainly, his foundation, The National Federation of Spiritual Healers,

---

[2]Christians recognize that the healing miracles of the Old Testament like those of Elijah and Elisha were also divine healing, being the activity of the Spirit of God. They were, however, only samples of what was more fully to be portrayed in Jesus Christ.

is very strong in the United Kingdom and Spiritist Healing Tabernacles are dotted about all over the country. Sometimes they prominently portray pictures of Jesus as "the Light of the World," which only adds to the confusion between spiritist, occult healing, and the divine healing ministered by the Christian church.

Divine healing is the activity of God in and through the person of Jesus Christ. It is not simply a matter of faith. It is certainly not the result of the activity of spirits whether thought of as human, angelic, or demonic. By such mediumistic activity people, in fact, unwittingly open themselves to the supernatural power of the devil who often heals the body in order to ensnare the soul. Divine healing involves the healing of the whole person—spirit, soul, mind, and body through a right relationship with God in Jesus Christ. Faith, for the Christian, is such a trusting and resting in the God revealed to us by Jesus, that we open our whole beings to the invasion of His Holy, health-giving Spirit. It is based upon a deep, personal relationship with God. This produces a healing that culminates in heaven, where we shall find ourselves perfectly restored in the whole of our beings. This is to the goal of the loving action of God, in a life fully yielded to Him.

I have constantly had to speak out in public about this vital distinction and stress the essential difference between divine healing and its many counterfeits. One of my first appearances on television was to refute occult practices which had been given media backing, to declare the exclusiveness of Jesus, the depth of His healing and the glories of His kingdom.

An Important Distinction

Every meeting I have held has focused on worshiping the glorified Jesus and proclaiming the necessity of responding to His love. An altar call for salvation, followed by careful counseling of converts, has always preceded ministry to the sick. I have always emphasized that I am engaged in *divine healing*, and have expounded its distinctive nature. Often this has brought criticism from commentators who have felt that all men of good will should join together in a ministry like this. Many spiritualists have attended my meetings thinking them to be the same as their own healing activities. However, they have soon been faced with the difference! Praise God, because I have never compromised on the issue, I have had the joy of seeing thousands of people find Jesus Christ as their Lord and Savior—the ultimate in supernatural experience.

Now that we have made this vital distinction, we are in a position to study the subject of divine healing in depth. As we do so we shall see more and more that, although its character is essentially supernatural, it still makes sense in an age of reason.

PART TWO

FOUNDATION TRUTHS

4

Sickness as Jesus Saw It

Most people recognize Jesus as one of the greatest teachers in history. The Sermon on the Mount is a monumental code of ethics, towering above everything ever taught about human attitudes and behavior. The example of the actual life and love of Jesus, culminating in His self-sacrifice, also makes sense in the world today. It shines like a light amid the darkness of the selfishness and strife which soil the pages of human history. This has been the Jesus predominantly presented from our pulpits and taught in our schools in the last decades. There is nothing particularly offensive about Jesus' actual life and teaching. However, the *supernaturalism* of Jesus is a real stumbling block to belief in Him in a rationalistic age like ours.

For this reason, many Christians have tried to rob the Gospels of their supernatural content. They have done this in order to try to make Jesus' ministry more acceptable to our modern era. This has reached a new extreme in Britain where some leading Christian professors recently wrote a book entitled *The Myth of God*

Incarnate, denying the miracle that God became man in Jesus.

However, it is an undeniable fact that the writers of the Gospels, in presenting a full and honest picture of Jesus of Nazareth, saw Him as a figure who was as equally at home in the supernatural realm as He was in the natural one. They show Him as a person for whom the distinction between natural and supernatural didn't even exist. He literally moved in God and, moment by moment, was empowered by the Holy Spirit. The very term "Messiah" means "the Anointed One." It was, therefore, as natural for Him to cure a leper as to talk about a sower; as natural for Him to still a storm as to fall asleep in a boat; as natural to cast out demons, as to teach in synagogues. When all our twentieth-century naturalistic bias has been put aside, we will find this is the real Jesus of history.

It is important for us to grasp the supernaturalism of the ministry of Jesus Christ because divine healing today is fundamentally an extension of His ministry. It is rooted and grounded in the New Testament record of His nature, His life, and His mission to mankind. Its origins, aims, and methods are entirely and exclusively biblical. For this reason, all who engage in divine healing ministry, or seek its blessings, must study and accept the way Jesus both diagnosed and met the needs of the men and women whom He encountered two thousand years ago.

Jesus' ministry began when He "returned in the power of the Spirit into Galilee. . . . And he came to Nazareth . . . and he went to the synagogue. . . . and there was given to him the book of the prophet Isaiah. He opened the book and found the place where it was written, 'The

Spirit of the Lord is upon me, because he has anointed me to preach good news to the poor. He has sent me to proclaim release to the captives and recovering of sight to the blind, to set at liberty those who are oppressed, to proclaim the acceptable year of the Lord' " (Luke 4:14-19).

It is very important to appreciate why Jesus chose this particular passage at the very outset of His ministry. It, in fact, was the blueprint, the plan of campaign, the *aim* of His whole ministry. A careful study of the events in the three years leading up to His crucifixion, shows Jesus carrying out this program to the very last detail.

Jesus saw His first task as "preaching the good news (the gospel) to the poor." He came preaching the gospel of God, and saying, "The time is fulfilled, and the kingdom of God is at hand; repent, and believe in the gospel" (Mark 1:14-15). His most vital, urgent, and fundamental task was to proclaim to spiritually destitute people both the reality of God's kingdom and the immediate possibility of entering it.

He was God's ambassador, announcing a free and absolute pardon to a rebellious human race. Because of His coming there was a new possibility of the "spiritually" sick, the lost, the religious outcasts, bringing their lives under the rule of God.

Jesus saw, from the beginning, that the Pharisees and other religionists of His day would not accept this message. This was because they already felt that they had "made it" with God (Matt. 23). Therefore, He spent most of His time with the tax collectors, harlots, and the other "sinners"—those who felt themselves spiritually poverty-stricken. He told the Pharisees that such as these would enter into the kingdom of God before they would (Luke 18:10-14).

The parable of the prodigal son best sums up this preaching of the good news to the poor (Luke 15). Its message was interpreted by Charles Wesley as:

> Outcasts of men to you I call
> Harlots and publicans and thieves.
> His open arms embrace you all
> Sinners alone His grace receive
> No need of Him the righteous
> He came the lost, to seek and save.

All aspects of Jesus' healing ministry, therefore, were complementary and ancillary to His proclaiming the gospel of the kingdom—the forgiveness of sins and reconciliation to God. Jesus saw this to be the basic, deepest need of all men. It was the backcloth on which all His other healing work was painted, the very fabric out of which His mission to mankind was woven. He never separated the rest of His healing work from the message of the kingdom as occultists and other religions, of necessity, must do. It follows that divine healing is all about the kingdom of God, and about the reconciliation of man to his Creator. It is seen in its proper perspective when it is intrinsically related to the *total* Christian message.

One important aspect of Jesus' message about the kingdom was that He claimed *himself* to have power on earth to forgive sins. He demonstrated His authority by showing its results in the realm of physical healing. This was in the case of a man so paralyzed that he had to be carried to Jesus on a stretcher by four friends (Luke 5:17-26). Jesus said to the sick person, "Man, your sins are forgiven you."

Despite protests from the Pharisees that these words were blasphemous, the declaration of Jesus was accepted by the man and resulted in his immediately getting to his feet. He picked up the bed on which he had just been carried and went home glorifying God.

The connection that can exist between sin and physical sickness is also implicit in Jesus' healing of another paralyzed man, this time at the pool of Bethesda. After performing the miracle, Jesus said, "See, you are well! Sin no more, that nothing worse befall you" (John 5:14).

There can be no doubt that the healing, forgiving love of God, which flowed through Jesus' very being, was also the positive factor in the remaking of the lives of demon-possessed people like Mary Magdalene (Mark 16:9), and many other distraught souls.

Throughout His life, Jesus was constantly preaching good news to the poor and the power of this message in bringing healing to the whole person cannot be overemphasized.

This brings us to the second aspect of the mission of Jesus, described in our key passage as "preaching deliverance to the captives." This is obviously a reference to the exorcism ministry which Jesus so frequently had to perform. His ministry in fact had hardly begun when "immediately there was in their synagogue a man with an unclean spirit; and he cried out, 'What have you to do with us, Jesus of Nazareth? Have you come to destroy us? I know who you are, the Holy One of God' " (Mark 1:23-27).

Jesus cried, " 'Be silent, and come out of him!' And the unclean spirit, convulsing him and crying with a loud voice, came out of him. And they were all amazed, so that they questioned among themselves, saying: 'What is this? A new teaching! With authority he commands even the unclean spirits, and they obey him' " (Mark 1:25-27).

It was, in fact, the *authority* of Jesus which so often startled the crowds. Demonic forces which held men in such terrible captivity acknowledged His superior status and had to yield to His word of command.

The New Testament record of Jesus' ministry is full of such incidents.

Although so often the explicit reference is to demonic forces and unclean spirits, as the instruments used by Satan to ensnare and possess men, yet Jesus' deliverance ministry opposed all alien domination of human life. Included in this category we would put fear, vice, and false religion. His statement was, "If the Son makes you free, you will be free indeed" (John 8:36). Paul reiterated this truth when he said, "Where the Spirit of the Lord is, *there* is freedom" (2 Cor. 3:17, italics mine).

It is interesting to notice also how often it was the spoken *word* of Jesus which brought release to the person.

This spiritual freedom which Jesus brought often had immediate beneficial effects upon the mind and body. A man out of whom Jesus drove a legion of demons is described as, "Sitting at the feet of Jesus, clothed and in his *right mind*" (Luke 8:35, italics mine).

Exorcism ministry also brought an end, among other things, to epilepsy, deafness, dumbness, blindness, and even a spinal complaint. (See *Supernatural Superpowers.*)

Jesus came to call men into a kingdom under the rule of God "whose service is perfect freedom."

The next realm of healing in the text from which Jesus preached was *the "recovering of sight to the blind."* This can legitimately be extended to include all physically sick, infirm, and incapacitated people.

Jesus was even more famous as a healer of sick bodies than he was either as a teacher or deliverer. One can hardly turn a page of the gospel story of His ministry without finding Him at work in this field. Many instances of healing are recorded in vivid detail and show that healings ranged from incapacities like lameness, blindness, and deafness to sicknesses like epilepsy, and hemorrhages, and even included death itself.

Sicknesses like these must have abounded in days when physicians had very little knowledge and only rudimentary medicines and techniques at their disposal.

It is not surprising, therefore, that Jesus was so overwhelmed by the pressing needs of the sick that He sometimes asked healed people not to tell anyone about their cures (Mark 1:43-44). But it was impossible to keep them quiet and so mass healing meetings frequently ensued.

"That evening, at sundown, they brought to him all who were sick or possessed with demons. And the whole city was gathered together about the door. And he healed many who were sick with various diseases, and cast out many demons" (Mark 1:32-34).

The people recognized him, and ran about the whole

neighborhood and began to bring sick people on their pallets to any place where they heard he was. And wherever he came, in villages, cities, or country, they laid the sick in the market places, and besought him that they might touch even the fringe of his garment; and as many as touched it were made well" (Mark 6:54-56).

What moving scenes these must have been!

Jesus declared also that He had come *"to set at liberty those who were bruised."* Who were these people?

We are bruised physically when we are dealt a hard blow on a bone. For days, or even weeks afterwards, the bruised area is very sensitive and we tend to jump with pain whenever it is touched. Protection becomes the order of the day!

Jesus, however, certainly was not referring to a simple, yet painful, *physical* affliction of this sort. He was describing a *spiritual* and *mental* condition wherein people can be "bruised" deep down, in their minds, personalities, or souls. The world then, as now, was full of people suffering from such deep hurt—bruised and, therefore, sensitive within; wounded and perhaps even bleeding to death in their innermost beings.

Few people escape such "knocks" if they live any length of time. We can be deeply hurt by other people, by their deeds or harsh words. We can be bashed about by the changes and chances, the circumstances of this transitory life, until we feel that we can hardly take any more. Failure and frustration also can deal us deadly blows. Jesus must constantly have been meeting such deeply hurt people who needed inner healing.

Bruised people tend to build a protective wall around

themselves, to withdraw from real, open involvement with other people. The real self rarely emerges. Relating to others at depth becomes difficult or almost impossible for them. They would find community life to be like a perpetual torture chamber. They have been dealt so many blows that they are frightened to come out of their protective armor. They become experts at defense mechanisms and evasive answers, being very difficult to reach. A chance word or action may unwittingly touch a sore point and result in reactions that could be either violently offensive or withdrawing and protective. The gospel of our Lord Jesus Christ reaches into the very depths of our beings and is addressed to the needs of people such as these.

Finally, it is interesting to turn back to the original passage in Isaiah which Jesus quoted and find there the words, "He has sent me to *bind up the brokenhearted*" (Isa. 61:1). Surely Jesus did not intend to exclude this category of need from the realm of His mission and ministry.

In both Greek and Hebrew, the languages of the Bible, the word "heart" means the "inner core" of the person, his very personality. It especially relates to the seat of his emotions. "Broken-hearted" people include those whom we today describe as "heartbroken," smashed within by grief and sorrow. But it has an even more profound meaning. Biblical broken-heartedness refers to the *personality* which has collapsed and fragmented under strain and pressure which has proved too heavy for it to bear. Many of the people we refer to as schizophrenic or psychotic fall into this biblical category.

When a person's body is sick, it produces symptoms like pain and discomfort which are signs to show that all is not well. The symptoms of "heart-brokenness," the "caving-in" of the personality, are emotions such as extreme fear, depression, tension, or obsessions. In biblical terminology the sickness that occurred when I was a teen-ager would have been described as "heart-brokenness." Today we use the term "neurosis" to describe this form of sickness.

Who knows what stories of rejection and heartache lay behind the lives of such people as Mary Magdalene, Zacchaeus, Thomas, Peter, and many others whom Jesus saved, to whom He brought wholeness? Certainly Jesus would penetrate their need, for He knew what was in man and brought the Good News of the binding up, the integration of shattered personalities.

Jesus, then, brought a gospel for the healing of the *whole* person. That is the true "full salvation" of the Christian religion. It relates to every possible aspect and need of human life. God created man in his entirety and it is in his entirety that He redeems him.

Jesus actually went *out* among men with His ministry. His was a continual healing mission. Every individual He met was of unique importance to Him, and was seen as a child of God in need. Jesus never refused anyone, He never turned anyone away. He moved towards the needs of men, and Christians believe that in His risen, glorified status He does so still today.

Furthermore, He always knew the area in which He had to minister. He did not meet the sick or broken-hearted as necessarily demon-possessed, for that would not have dealt with the source of their problems, but would have only bruised them more. Like the master physician of souls He truly was, He quickly diagnosed the real cause of a person's disease, and dealt with it. Perhaps occasionally then, as now, He had to hurt in order to heal. All, however, who truly trusted Him and opened their lives to Him were transformed, as Paul would say "from faith to faith" and "glory to glory" (2 Cor. 3:18).

Despite all the good work of the medical profession, the spiritually destitute, Satan's captives, the bruised, the sick, and the broken-hearted still abound in their thousands today. Multitudes of them flock to meetings where the risen Jesus Christ still manifests His presence and compassion. The needs which have been presented to me have been as deep and as various as in the days of Jesus. I have asked Him to show me the area in which to minister His healing love. As His grace has flooded human hearts, we have experienced that the Spirit of the Lord is upon *us*, anointing us to:

Preach good news to the poor . . .
Proclaim release to the captives . . .
Recovering of sight to the blind . . .
Set at liberty those who are oppressed . . .
Proclaim the acceptable year of the Lord.

(Luke 4:18)

5

The Supernatural Ministry of Jesus of Nazareth

Doctors readily acknowledge that physical sickness, inner bruising and heart-brokenness are still very prevalent in the world today. A few psychiatrists even admit the reality of demon possession. However, to modern medical practitioners Jesus' actual healing methods seem incredibly bizarre and unreal. For instance, it is recorded that when dealing with a condition of high fever, Jesus "rebuked the fever, and it left her" (Luke 4:39).

Jesus treated the sickness as a personal entity which could hear His words and obey them! This is hardly a method prescribed in contemporary medical dictionaries! Jesus seems to have been reprimanding an evil life-force which He saw to be underlying the symptoms of the fever. He exercised spiritual authority over it and drove it away!

Certainly, although Jesus' methods always brought rapid results, they take a lot of understanding from the point of view of modern medical science. His approach to the cause and cure of sickness was always *supernatural*.

The use of the spoken word in healing is characteristic

of Jesus' healing ministry. Sometimes, as we have seen, He addressed a demon; sometimes healing came when He pronounced a sinner to be forgiven. Usually, however, He actually addressed the sick *person* as in the case of the man with the withered hand.

Jesus commanded, "Come here. . . . Stretch out your hand" (Mark 3:3-5). As the man obeyed, his hand was restored.

Jesus not only spoke His words of command in religious buildings but on streets and hillsides or wherever the need arose. Luke records that it was while passing through a village that He met ten lepers, who, as the law demanded, stood at a distance.

They implored, "Jesus, Master, have mercy on us" (Luke 17:13). When He saw them He simply said, "Go and show yourselves to the priests. And as they went they were cleansed" (Luke 17:14).

Once again, obedience to the command of Jesus brought healing.

The eyes of a blind man were opened as he was actually sitting by the wayside, begging. On this occasion Jesus said, "Receive your sight" (Luke 18:42).

And immediately he could see. Such was the power of Jesus' words.

It was by the power of His word that Jesus healed people *at a distance.* Usually it was important that the sick actually came to Jesus in order to receive His ministry direct. But distance was no barrier to the supernaturalism of the Messiah. This was so when Jesus was asked to heal a centurion's servant who was at death's door. As Jesus approached the house, the centurion sent servants to Him with the message, "Lord, do not trouble yourself, for I am not worthy to have you come under my roof . . . But *say the word*, and let my servant be healed" (Luke 7:6-7, italics mine).

When Jesus heard this he " marveled at him" and said to the multitude that followed Him "I tell you, not even in Israel have I found such faith" (Luke 7:9). And when those who had been sent returned to the house, they found the slave well.

Greater distances than this were involved in the healing of a nobleman's son (John 4:46), and a Canaanite woman's daughter (Matt. 15:22). Again it was the power of Jesus' word, effective over miles of distance, which brought healing to the sick.

Jesus even spoke the word of life to the dead, those obviously in the ultimate condition of being incapable of response! And yet, it was in this way that Lazarus of Bethany was restored to his sisters (John 11:17-44); a widow received her only son back from the dead, while the funeral procession was actually in progress (Luke 7:11-17); and a ruler of a synagogue found himself having to prepare a meal for a daughter he had just seen die (Luke 8:55). What could be more supernatural than this?

It is apparent also from the biblical record that Jesus' use of His *hands* was as much a feature of His healing ministry as the use of His lips. Often, however, the two were combined. When healing a leper He reached out to touch the "untouchable" as He said, "I will; be clean" (Mark 1:41). Immediately the leprosy left him.

Often Jesus actually touched the part of the body which was afflicted. Hence, He put his fingers into the ears of a deaf man, saying "Ephphatha . . . Be opened" (Mark 7:34). He also touched his tongue to heal him of his dumbness. (See also Matthew 20:34.)

More frequently, however, the New Testament tells us that He simply laid His hands upon them and healed them all. Perhaps on these occasions His hands were placed upon the head, as representing the whole body.

On one occasion the touch was in reverse. A woman reached out of the crowd and touched the hem of His garment.

"For she said, 'If I touch even his garments, I shall be made well.' And immediately the hemorrhage ceased; and she felt in her body that she was healed of her disease" (Mark 5:28-29).

In fact, Jesus used all sorts of methods in His healing ministry. In one case of blindness He healed a man by covering his eyes with a paste made of His spittle and clay, telling him to wash it off in the pool of Siloam (John 9:1-12). Oil, too, a medicine of the time, but also a symbol of the Holy Spirit, was often used to anoint the sick people (Mark 6:13). The result was healing way beyond anything normally expected of the medication!

These and other detailed incidents show clearly that Jesus gave every case of sickness His personal, individual attention. Although He often had to deal with vast crowds of people, He used no mass method. Neither did He have a ritualistic formula for dealing with everyone in an identical manner. He was sensitive to every different need and the precise method to be used in meeting it. This meant also His being in constant communion with the Father, the source of all supernatural knowledge, love, and power. Every healing, therefore, was the work of the Holy Trinity. The Father was the source of the healing, Jesus the instrument, and the Holy Spirit the power. In this way God's perfect will for each of His children was wonderfully effected.

So intense was His interest in every individual case that Jesus often spent hours in personal counseling. We are given examples of this in His conversation with Nicodemus (John 3), His encounter with the woman of Samaria (John 4), and His dealing with Zacchaeus (Luke 19:1-10). These were life-transforming occasions. In the case of the woman, we have a vivid portrayal of that supernaturalism of Jesus, which, for Him, was so very natural.

"You are right in saying, 'I have no husband'; for you have had five husbands, and he whom you now have is not your husband," He told the startled woman (John 4:17-18).

This supernatural revelation led to her realizing that Jesus was Messiah, and further to many Samaritans from that city believing in Him because of the woman's testimony. "He told me all that I ever did" (John 4:39).

Jesus was given, through the Spirit, supernatural wisdom, knowledge, faith, discernment, healing ability, and the power to work miracles, all of which were used for the glory of God and the meeting of the needs of mankind. (See 1 Corinthians 12:3-10.)

One might well ask why all these methods were necessary to supernaturalism. Why didn't healings just simply happen? In answering this question we reach deep into the ways in which God, an invisible, infinite, spiritual

Being deals with the creatures He has made. In His wisdom He has given us five ways of apprehending reality. These are the senses of sight, hearing, touch, taste, and smell. Quite simply, these are the only ways in which anything can be real to us. For this reason, in order that we might know Him, He had to make himself available to our senses. So, "The Word became flesh and dwelt among us, full of grace and truth; we have beheld His glory" (John 1:14).

In Jesus, God conditioned himself to our senses. We know God in and through the person of Jesus, "the image of the invisible God" (Col. 1:15).

This principle also applies to the activity of God in the divine healing ministry. If we are to receive supernatural healing power from God, it must come to us through the gateway of our senses.

The fact that God uses "outward and visible signs" as means of communicating "inward and spiritual grace" is an age-long insight of Christian theology. Upon it rests much of the worship and devotion of the Christian Church, including all of the sacraments. In order that man could receive supernatural healing, therefore, Jesus had, of necessity, to speak words into their ears, perform deeds that they could see, and use His hands and other material aids to make contact through the sense of touch.

Jesus' ministry was essentially and undeniably supernatural. It had to be, in order to meet men's deepest needs. It was, however, through the gateway of the senses that He communicated that which was otherwise beyond human comprehension. The results can only be described as miraculous. All He said and did brought an invasion of the power of an almighty, all-loving God, into the weaknesses, sicknesses, and frailties of human lives.

Today's ministry of divine healing is an extension of the ministry of Jesus as recorded in the Gospels. The methods I have used, therefore, have inevitably been based upon His. Christians are rightly suspicious that those who use other ways are not truly ministering divine healing. The New Testament is still the one textbook from which divine healing must ultimately be derived for ministry in the world today. It has been read at all of my Power, Praise, and Healing meetings and my every word and deed has been weighed by its message and methods. Divine healing ministry today must be fundamentally and absolutely biblical.

6

Supernatural but Very Personal

The source of Jesus' healing power was His deep personal relationship with His Father. Those who sought His ministry were healed, not because He applied right techniques, but because they came into real, personal, contact with Him, the Son of God. Only then did the supernatural power of God reach them through the words and actions of the Messiah, the "anointed One." Divine healing today, likewise, always involves an *encounter* with Jesus!

This needs to be explained to us because we have been conditioned to look for definite, predictable, and quick results from our efforts in every sphere of life. We regard progress as a matter of finding better techniques to achieve our objectives. We are, therefore, prone also to think that divine healing is simply a matter of right methods which will *of themselves* produce easy, instantaneous results at any "miracle service" we want to arrange!

The *methods* of divine healing, however, are very secondary to communion with a living, loving, acting God.

Divine healing miracles *do* happen but they are never simply the result of the right "know-how"; they flow from the intervention of an almighty, personal God acting to meet the needs of those who respond to His love and enter into a deep relationship with Him in Jesus (John 14:6). Those who approach divine healing mainly as a matter of technique will inevitably be disillusioned, but those who come expecting great things from God will never be disappointed. He is not limited, as we are, by the laws of the natural order, but "is able to do far more abundantly than all that we ask or think" (Eph. 3:20), according to the power at work within us.

Divine healing, then, *is* supernatural, but it is *not magical*. Its results can never be limited to the *rational* laws and techniques of medical science and it is equally important that it is never confused with the *irrational* incantations and rituals of magic. In magic the correct words and deeds are thought to have power, *in themselves* to accomplish miracles; God, in such cases, is almost superfluous! The attraction of witch doctors, ancient and modern, is that they are thought to have access to secret rites and ceremonies which can channel supernatural power in any direction. When they seem to be successful, it is not because they have a deep relationship with God, but simply that they know the correct supernatural spells to use. Obviously such superstition and recourse to the irrational is the devil's playground.

Satan often even traps Christians into looking for magic to bring about healing. I have known some Christians who place such an emphasis on correct *ritual* that they have unconsciously come dangerously near to the magical. Others pursue ministers who they think are more "powerful" than the average, without realizing that their attitudes are precariously near the way in which people have turned to witch doctors. Jesus' ministry shows us the falsity and danger of all beliefs in the efficacy of magic. We must keep on emphasizing that the secret of *His* success was the deep personal relationship He enjoyed with His Father. This union of being was the source of His supernatural, loving power. Although He used physical methods to communicate God's grace, yet His ministry clearly shows that divine healing is, in essence, profoundly *personal*.

It follows that the minister of divine healing today should always be a person whose deep communion with Jesus Christ is apparent to all whom he meets. People must meet Jesus through him. He must, therefore, in his own spiritual life, seek an ever deeper relationship with his Lord. As Jesus himself often had to go away from people to seek the presence of His heavenly Father, so those who serve Him today in the demanding work of healing the sick will often have to get away from the crowds to be alone with God.

I discovered this truth the hard way. As the number of meetings I was taking multiplied rapidly, so the demands of desperate, needy people became incessant and I felt I just could not refuse them. In the end I became sick myself. Utterly exhausted, I had to cancel a whole month of meetings. I lay in bed weak and ill, wondering how it could ever have happened to me.

When I recovered, I went away to a convent for a

retreat in order to be entirely alone with the Lord. For three days I communicated with no one but Him. He showed me that my ministry had become powerless and almost mechanical because people had been allowed to come in the way of my relationship with Him. Hence I had lost my peace and become almost only a performer.

I repented at depth and, after a period of hours of communion with Him every day, I found my soul again knit with His soul, in deep love. I had learned a profound spiritual lesson.

Jesus himself warned, "On that day, many will say to me, 'Lord, Lord, did we not prophesy in your name, and cast out demons in your name, and do many mighty works in your name?' And then will I declare to them, 'I never *knew* you; depart from me, you evildoers" (Matt. 7:22-23, italics mine).

Knowing Jesus therefore is the all-important factor. Since that time of trial, my continual prayer has been: "Lord, do not let people merely see *me*. Let me be so transparent that they will, as I minister, see only *you*." I have been so grateful for letters which have assured me that, even when assailed by critics on television, the peace and love of Jesus have shone through my life. Were it ever to be otherwise my ministry would simply be, at best, a matter of technique, and, at worst, simply magic.

Sometimes, after successful healing meetings, I have been asked, "How do you do it? Can you give me the secret?"

At such times I have sensed that the inquirers have fallen into the trap of looking for my "secret techniques."

There are, in fact, no methods which can in any way

substitute for a deep, personal walk with Christ, ever-increasing sensitivity to His presence, and a clearer hearing of His voice. Everyone to whom we minister must come into contact not with us, but with the Jesus who is at work in us and through us, and be blessed by *Him*.

The vital importance of this encounter with God is clearly demonstrated in the New Testament. There we see that every healing received *from* Jesus involved some definite personal contact *with Him*. The furthest extremity allowed was the "hem of His garment." One woman actually said, "If I only touch his garment, I shall be made well" (Matt. 9:21; see also Mark 6:56).

Jesus, however, wanted a more personal relationship with her so, after she had made the "touch," and He had sensed that healing power had gone from Him, He insisted that she should be found and brought to Him.

Tremblingly, she admitted what she had done. Then Jesus gave her the *real* reason why she had been healed. It was not a magic touch, but *her faith* which had made her whole (Mark 5:25-34).

Faith is, in fact, the basis of all our personal relationships. It is involved in all our friendships, and is a prime factor in marriage. "Faith" or "trust" is also the basis of a good relationship between *parents and children*. How much more than does our relationship with God involve complete faith in Him!

It is for this reason that Scripture tells us, "Without faith it is impossible to please him [God]. For whoever would draw near to God must believe that he exists and that he rewards those who seek him" (Heb. 11:6).

Jesus taught that our faith in approaching God must

have the simplicity of little children coming to their father for his gifts. "Unless you turn and become like children, you will never enter the kingdom of heaven" (Matt. 18:3). "Suffer little children . . . to come unto me: for of such is the kingdom of heaven" (Matt. 19:14 KJV).

So, Jesus taught we must ask God for healing in the simple trust that He will give all that is good to His children. He said, "When ye pray, say, *Our Father*" (Luke 11:2 KJV, italics mine). And, "If you then, who are evil, know how to give good gifts to your children, how much more will your Father who is in heaven give good things to those who ask him" (Matt. 7:11). "Ask, and it will be given you" (Matt. 7:7).

Real faith, therefore, means unquestioning certainty that God will definitely give us all that is good for us. Jesus' words give us a key definition of faith: "Therefore I tell you, whatever you ask in prayer, believe that you receive it, and it will be yours" (Mark 11:24).

We have already said that divine healing has to be differentiated from faith healing. This is so when faith is thought of as some magical or psychological device, which will, of *itself*, produce healing. Now, however, we see how important faith is as a basis for our relationship with God. It is through this relationship, based on unquestioning faith, that God moves to heal.

It is for this reason that Jesus always looked for faith when He was ministering to men's needs. He said to one man, "Do you believe that I am able to do this?" (Matt. 9:28). On another occasion he declared, "All things are possible to him who believes" (Mark 9:23). Of a centurion He said, "I have not found so great faith, no, not in Israel"

(Luke 7:9 KJV). To a healed leper, to blind Bartimaeus, and to the woman who came out of the crowd, He said, "Thy faith hath made thee whole" (Luke 17:19 KJV).

Jesus went to extremes in declaring what could be effected when one had faith in God's love and power. "For verily I say unto you, That whosoever shall say unto this mountain, Be thou removed, and be thou cast into the sea; and shall not doubt in his heart, but shall believe that those things which he saith shall come to pass; he shall have whatsoever he saith" (Mark 11:23 KJV).

Far too often *our* faith is like that of a lady who had a mountain of rubbish in front of her window. It obscured her view and made her house dark. She decided to act upon this promise of Jesus about moving mountains.

"Mountain!" she shouted. "I command you to go into the Atlantic Ocean! In the name of the Lord—go!" And she went to bed.

The next morning she got out of bed and pulled back the curtain, only to find the offending obstacle still firmly rooted there. Turning to her husband she said, "There you are. Just as I thought! It's still there!"

So often, when people are not healed, we are thinking, albeit below the level of consciousness, "He's still sick, *just as I thought.*" This can, unfortunately, be an echo of the sick person's own unconscious doubt. "I am not healed, just as I thought!"

Real faith is simply taking it for granted that God will do as He has promised.

We are used to exercising this sort of faith in *people* in the ordinary events of life. For instance, when we are guests in a home, we take it for granted that our hosts have provided a bed which is in good condition. Without thinking, we lift our feet off the floor and commit our whole body to its care. What a shock we would get if the bed were to part in the middle and we were to fall to the floor! When real, subconscious faith is let down it always results in a shock. The more absolute the faith, the more terrible the shock! Yet few people are really shocked when someone is not miraculously healed! This is because basically they never really expected them to be so!

Our prayers are so often that of the father who came to Jesus saying: "I believe; help thou mine unbelief" (Mark 9:24 KJV). Yet for effective results in divine healing we must believe that God, our Father, is both able and willing to heal all those who come to Him.

I have found that people, in fact, often confuse "faith" with *sincerity*. Someone may, however, be a "sincere" Christian, without necessarily having "faith" in God for healing.

Sometimes also "faith" is confused with "hope." We *hope* we will be healed. We *hope* our loved one will recover. Hope, however, is always related to the future; faith grasps the certainty of the *present*. The Bible says, "Faith is the assurance of things hoped for, the conviction of things not seen" (Heb. 11:1). Lord, give us this faith!

The New Testament record shows us that when we do have such faith, it can, in fact, be exercised vicariously; that is, we can have faith in God for the healing of someone else—and the miracle will happen! So it was when Jesus saw the faith of his *four friends* that He said to the paralyzed man, "Arise, and take up they bed, and walk" (Mark 2:9 KJV).

Their faith in Jesus' power to heal had been expressed even to breaking a hole through a roof in order to get their friend into His presence.

Likewise, it was the centurion's superabundant faith in the spiritual authority of Jesus that brought healing to his dying slave.

To believe in God for "supernatural" healing is very difficult for people like us, who are children of a scientific, rationalistic age. Perhaps "being too ignorant to know what is impossible" is an advantage after all when it comes to receiving divine healing! Certainly the Western world is, generally speaking, skeptical in this respect. But, as we have seen, we *are* living in days of a recovery of belief in the supernatural. To Christians is given the task of making sure by life, teaching, and example, that this faith finds its proper object—a personal relationship with God through Jesus Christ. Then divine healing miracles will abound!

The Bible teaches us, therefore, that there are no shortcuts to supernatural power. Divine healing involves a personal relationship with Jesus Christ. This is because healing flows from God himself. We meet *this* God only in Jesus (John 14:6). People seeking the divine healing cannot bypass an encounter with God *based on faith* in His Son, Jesus Christ.

In the gospel record sick people actually *coming to* Jesus showed that at least the beginnings of faith were there, and on such faith Jesus could act in power!

The story of the healing of the man at the Pool of Bethesda (see John 5) illustrates this in a somber as well as a joyous way. I had often wondered why Jesus healed only one of the many sick people who were there that day. It was so unlike Him! Then I realized that they were all staring intently *at the pool*, waiting for that rare moving of the water, which brought the possibility of healing. Only one man actually turned to look at Jesus and thereby became involved with *Him*. Likewise, today there can be no healing while people are concentrating purely on the magical or the superstitious. Divine healing is for those who "turn their eyes upon Jesus and look full in His wonderful face." Encounter with Christ is vital. It is the beginning and end of faith.

Another interesting factor in this story is the way in which Jesus asked the lame man the question: "Do you want to be healed?" (John 5:6).

The answer seems obvious. For what other reason would the man be sitting at the pool every day? Couldn't Jesus take it for granted that a sick man wanted to be well? Apparently not!

"Do you *really* want to be made well?" is a real question for us all to face. Psychologists today know that a neurotic person can, subconsciously, be holding onto his sickness, despite the torment, because the symptoms are serving an ulterior motive. Perhaps they are a cover-up for a feeling of failure, or an expression of inability to face up to the pressures of life. The sickness substitutes for the real problem and enables the afflicted person, albeit at great price, to avoid life's responsibilities. Recovery from mental illness, even from a natural point of view, begins with the sufferer, *without qualification*, desiring to be well.

The same can be true of physical illness. It can almost

become part of a person's way of life to be ill; part of their personality sickness can be the crutch on which they lean. If this is so, there is a subconscious desire still to be sick. In such cases, the healing of one illness is rapidly followed by the onset of another.

In pointing out this truth, which Jesus so clearly taught, we must be careful not to accuse *every* unhealed sick person, or even *most* such people, of the desire to remain ill. We must also point out that there is a real difference between subconscious motivation and deliberate malingering. However, this question which Jesus asked, "Do you *want* to be made well?" reinforces the truth that divine healing is not magical. Because it is *personal*, an unqualified desire to be well is a very important factor in healing. He will never violate our wills—we must want God to heal us with *all* our beings—and then He will.

Faith, desire, and *obedience* are vital in receiving divine healing. Naaman the leper had to learn this, centuries before Christ (2 Kings 5:1-14). He nearly was not healed because he refused to dip seven times in the Jordan. When he eventually obeyed, however, the miracle happened.

In the New Testament, it was when the man obeyed the command of Jesus, "Rise, take up your bed and walk!"; when the lepers turned and obeyed the command, "Go, show yourselves to the priests!"; when the blind man did as Jesus told him and went to "wash in the Pool of Siloam"—that they were all healed.

James says that "Faith without works is dead" (James 2:26 KJV).

True faith always issues in actions. Faith in a person is expressed in doing exactly as he says. Obedience is a vital part in divine healing because if we really have faith in the Lord, then we will *obey* Him, and begin both to confess and *act* our healing.

Once again, however, we must issue a caution. There is a great deal of difference between acting out of *faith* and acting out of *doubt*. The people who obeyed Jesus did so, taking it for granted that His healing word to them had come to pass. Today I have known people who have been so convinced, certain, sure, that they have been divinely healed, with every trace of their sickness having gone, that they have got out of wheelchairs or dispensed with medication. Glory to the Lord has abounded! However, I have also heard of some tragic cases where sick people acted in these ways "to see if it had worked" when they had not actually been convinced that they had been healed at all.

In such cases, when a person has even the slightest uncertainty, it is better to consult a sympathetic doctor for verification of the healing. Spurious healings do not glorify the Lord!

One last factor which must not be omitted is that an attitude of forgiveness is essential for God to move in our lives. Resentment, bitterness, and the "unforgiving spirit" are barriers to healing. Forgiveness brings a real release of soul and an openness to God. The necessity for the forgiving spirit was so often the burden of Jesus' message. He often taught it in relation to prevailing prayer.

"And forgive us our debts, as we forgive our debtors" is

a vital clause in the Lord's prayer (Matt. 6:12-14 KJV). Also, in the very passage where Jesus taught so much about faith moving mountains, He also said, "And whenever you stand praying, forgive, if you have anything against any one; so that your Father also who is in heaven may forgive you your trespasses" (Mark 11:25).

When Peter asked just what limit should be set upon a man's forgiveness of one who had repeatedly wronged him, he thought "seven times" was very generous. But Jesus said, "I do not say to you seven times, but seventy times seven" (Matt. 18:22).

Jesus then went on to tell a parable about the Father's unwillingness to forgive us our massive "debt" to Him, unless we are likewise prepared to forgive our brethren their comparatively trivial "debts" to us.

When we release people from their sins against us there is always a spiritual *rebound* effect. *We* are the people who benefit, for a profound and deep spiritual release takes place in *us*. It is as if our hands have been clenched, holding on to the soiled rags of our resentment. When we let go, they are then free to grasp the healing hand of God.

Divine healing is not magical. It will not *automatically* work for us, no matter how holy the minister may be, how "powerfully" he performs his task, and what techniques he may use. It is for this reason that he cannot just walk down the road healing everybody he sees, or go into the nearest hospital and empty it. Because divine healing is profoundly personal, a *response* is needed, and it is obviously in this area that a great deal of the reason for today's nonhealing lies.

Jesus, then, came to us; He appeared as God among

men, with a mission and a ministry to the whole person. This ministry was not scientific but rather unashamedly supernatural. He used methods whereby ordinary sense experience became the gateway to an invasion of the whole life by God's loving power. Jesus' ministry, however, was not magical. It flowed from a personal relationship with His Father. It necessitated an openness of the life in Him in faith, obedience, and love.

Today's ministry involves these same factors. Healing power flows not only through the response of the sick to the person of our Lord, but also through the deep communion the minister has with Him. In fact, the response to Jesus of *all* involved in fellowship with the sick person is also of great importance, whether it be relatives, friends or church congregation, for there can be barriers to healing in all these areas. But when there is a real, deep, personal response to our Lord, a real awareness of His presence and intense expectancy of what He will do, anything and everything can happen in the realm of healing. Divine healing *is* supernatural but, at the same time, very personal.

Got any rivers you think are uncrossable?
Got any mountains you can't tunnel through?
God specializes in things thought impossible.
He can do what no other can do.

The truth of this simple song has been proved in the lives of many thousands of people living today.

7

The Heart of the Matter

The focus of our attention so far has been upon the ways in which Jesus communicated supernatural power to meet the deepest needs of those who came to Him for help. Every pastor knows, however, that the problem of suffering *itself* is a great stumbling block in the way of people coming to belief in a benevolent Creator.

"Why have these children been born so terribly incapacitated?"

"Why is my dear wife suffering such unbearable pain with cancer?"

"Why was this woman's husband snatched away by death in the prime of life, leaving her alone to bring up her family?"

"Why did God allow that earthquake which wiped out thousands of people and which brought homelessness and suffering to thousands more destitute people?"

"Why doesn't He stop murders and wars?"

Such questions are constantly being asked of those engaged in the ministry of the church.

In my mission I have been brought into personal

contact with the needs of thousands of desperate people. This work is born of the compassion of Christ in one's heart. For me, people are not simply material for miracles; I feel intensely for them. Their conditions weigh upon my heart. As, from the platform, I have looked out upon women with incapacitated children in their arms, the handicapped supported by canes, and paralyzed people confined to wheelchairs, I have entered into something of the meaning of these words: "And Jesus . . . saw much people and was moved with compassion toward them" (Mark 6:34 KJV).

The problems raised for a Christian by the sufferings of many good people are inescapable. Underlying such intense, personal, and often heartbreaking situations are deep, spiritual issues which cannot be ignored.

Why do people suffer?

How can it be overcome?

When will it end?

Are we being prepared for some higher form of existence?

These issues are as relevant to life today as for any past generation.

Of course, for today's uncompromising humanist there is no such problem. They accept the view that, from the beginning, this planet had within it both the possibilities for human life to evolve, and the inherent dangers, diseases and disasters, which would threaten that life. They accept the theory that life was inevitably a matter of the survival of the fittest, most adaptable and most intelligent creatures. From this point of view "suffering" has simply to be accepted as an inevitable part of our natural existence. For scientists, the answer to suffering can only be found through understanding more about the laws governing our universe, and using the forces within it for the well-being of mankind. Humanists can, in fact, point to the undeniable successes the various medical sciences have had in alleviating suffering and pain.

While welcoming all these achievements, few people today are prepared to let the matter rest there. Exploring the depths of our universe cannot be left only to scientists. As the recent resurgence of supernaturalism demonstrates, men ask both spiritual and scientific questions, as they seek to plumb the meaning of their existence. They still ask, "Why do people suffer?"

In seeking to answer them, we are brought to the threshold of the deepest aspects of life. Even more, we enter into the very heart of God—His agonizing love.

It is because God is love that He did not make men and women simply to be robots. He made us in His own image with freedom of will. This is because love can only be satisfied with a relationship based on a free response from the beloved. This involved the terrible possibility that we might reject Him and take our love elsewhere—but it was a risk love had to take. God could do no other, because He is love at its highest, most noble, and best. The story of history is that human beings have consistently rejected God's offer of love and broken this relationship with Him.

From a Christian point of view, the ultimate cause of suffering is man's Fall—his rejection of God. Because of this, our love, which was meant to flow to God, has turned back upon ourselves. We have been self-centered instead of God-centered. Losing the unity given by our love for our heavenly Father, full of self-love, we have also turned against each other, making the world a continual economic, sociological, military, political and psychological battlefield. The Fall has resulted in a disease called sin which has affected the whole of humanity. It is now part of our very nature, and a direct cause of suffering.

Further, the Bible teaches that because of the deep spiritual relationship human beings have with the rest of the natural world, the whole created universe has been affected by the disease of sin.

"For we know that the whole creation has been groaning in travail together until now; and not only the creation, but we ourselves . . . groan inwardly" (Rom. 8:22-23).

This is why our environment seems so hostile and so many disasters occur. Men are still as spiritually desperate as ever. People are bruised and heartbroken by the actions of other sinners, or because of the pressures of a fallen world. It is because our bodies are part of a fallen, natural order that malformed children are born, and that we can become sick, infirm, and we eventually die. This ultimately is why people suffer. God, however, is love, and He has himself acted to overcome the results of our rebellion. He sent His Son, Jesus Christ, into the world, not only to minister to the needs of the people of His time, but also to die for all mankind.

It came as a terrible shock to the disciples when, in the midst of all the excitement, clamor and acclamation, Jesus began to say, "The Son of man *must* suffer many things, and be rejected by the elders and the chief priests and the scribes, and be killed, and after three days rise again" (Mark 8:31, italics mine).

Peter, especially, took great exception to these remarks. "Lord!" he said. "This shall never happen to you" (Matt. 16:22).

Jesus, however, went on to predict the peril which not only He, but also all faithful disciples, would face as they followed Him.

It is important to understand that the Greek word for "must" (*dei*), used in the context of Jesus' death, has the force of "compulsion," "inevitability," and "destiny." The crucifixion of Jesus was inevitable.

God's answer to the Fall of Man was, more and more, love. "God so loved the world that he gave his only Son" (John 3:16).

God, in fact, had never forsaken the human race, the creatures He made to love. He had sent messenger after messenger with a loving offer of reconciliation. The offer had, however, repeatedly been rejected. In the end, therefore, He sent His Son. He said, "They will reverence my son" (Matt. 21:37 KJV).

But, true to form, mankind even rejected Him. When we crucified Jesus we flung the love of God back in His face.

The cross shows God, in the midst of the suffering and pain which human beings continually bring upon themselves by rejecting Him. It speaks of a love that has to allow beloved men and women to suffer, despite the great agony caused to its own heart. It portrays a fantastic act of self-sacrificing love on the part of God, in which He himself drank, to the very dregs, the cup of all the physical, mental, and spiritual anguish mankind can endure. He could not put an end to it all, because to do so would be to deprive us of our freedom, to make puppets out of people, to deny His own love.

The cross shows the *continuing* love of God, blazing like a beacon, drawing like a magnet, pulling at the very heartstrings of every man, woman, and child. God has no power but the power of love, for God *is* love. "God was in Christ, reconciling the world unto himself" (2 Cor. 5:19 KJV).

Once again, we see the fundamental difference between divine healing and mere supernaturalism. Christianity is not simply about supernatural, impersonal power, whether mediated by so-called human "guides" on the other side, or by the incantations of witch doctors. Divine healing is all about love, offered by God to men. The offer of healing is focused on the crucifixion, which is at the heart of it all. Here our deepest sickness, sin, is clearly revealed as the rejection of our God. The cross is also a window into heaven, showing the agony of God sharing all our suffering, and bearing our sin. It reveals the love of God which will never let us go. It offers the possibility of a new healing relationship for *all* men of *all* time. It is the heart of the matter of divine healing.

But when will God bring suffering to an end? The blessing of God is that although *complete* healing may take this lifetime, or even beyond, our "spirit and soul and body [*will*] be preserved blameless unto *the coming of our Lord Jesus Christ*" (1 Thess. 5:23 KJV italics mine).

This is because God's act of salvation did not stop at the cross of Calvary; it went on in the resurrection of Jesus from the dead, and will finally be completed at His return to earth in triumphant glory.

It was the resurrection which transformed the death of Jesus from being simply another sad story, into the reality of a living hope for mankind. By raising Jesus from the dead, God showed that the whole course of events had been under His control; that the crucifixion had been *His* doing even more than that of the crowd.

The resurrection turned tragedy into triumph, despair into hope, darkness into light, and death into life. It showed that the ultimate destiny in which we are completely healed is *heaven. We are being prepared, even through suffering, for a higher form of existence.*

"We have been born anew to a living hope through the resurrection of Jesus Christ from the dead, and to an inheritance which is imperishable, undefiled, and unfading, kept in heaven for you, who by God's power are guarded through faith for a salvation ready to be revealed in the last time" (1 Pet. 1:3-5).

The resurrection is the greatest miracle of all time. It is also the central, foundation miracle of divine healing. The resurrection takes the ministry of Jesus from first-century Palestine into the twentieth century. Divine healing is possible today because Jesus is alive today! If Jesus had stayed in the tomb, divine healing would have been only past history; now it is a present reality!

The great miracle of the resurrection goes beyond the vague hopes of all other supernaturalism. It is a fact that, from time immemorial, men have hoped for immortality, life after death. It was for this reason that slaves were killed and, together with presents, were buried with the pharaohs. It was hoped they might all be of use to them in the after-life.

The phenomenal, unique fact in Jesus' survival after death was that *He took His body with Him.* This is the fundamental difference between mere "immortality" and the Christian truth of full resurrection. "Immortality" is the soul and spirit being set free from the body, its "evil," its "unworthy prison." Christianity, however, speaks about the resurrection *of the whole person,* as an individual: spirit, soul, mind, and body. This is full salvation. So, in the resurrection of Jesus, we see again why divine healing is the ministry of the gospel for the whole person. We see its ultimate aim—resurrection for each one of us, entire and complete. (See 1 Corinthians 15.)

The world today is still one of suffering humanity. We are living in a rationalistic, scientific, and, in many ways, a humanistic age. Despite the successes of man in our time, we are experiencing a resurgence of supernaturalism, perhaps born of despair, bewilderment, confusion, or even impatience with our failures to overcome our basic problems. Needs abound all around us and many are now seeking instant spiritual solutions. These, more often than not, they do not find.

In the last few years I have traveled along the highways of suffering; not my own, this time, but those of others. To set out on a divine healing mission has been to learn at first hand the depths of suffering in the world.

This is no shallow, superficial gamesmanship. This is no spiritual hit-and-run raid. We are dealing with desperate, suffering, vulnerable people.

The Heart of the Matter

I could not face this ministry were it not for the cross of Christ and all it portrays of God with us in the midst of suffering.

> Sharing their sorrow and shame,
> Seeking the lost,
> Saving, redeeming at measureless cost.
>
> (R. Walmsley)

> Hold Thou Thy Cross, before my closing eyes
> Shine through the gloom and point me to the skies.
> Heaven's morning breaks, and earth's vain shadows flee
> In life, in death, O Lord, abide with me.
>
> (H.F. Lyte)

On the cross the heart of God's love enters into, embraces, and bears man's suffering, for *all* time. "With His stripes we are healed" (Isa. 53:5).

Christians also eagerly look forward to the time when their risen and exalted Lord will return and bring that new, redeemed order for which Paul says the whole creation is groaning and waiting (Rom. 8:22-25). The only reason for delay is that God is still awaiting the response of more people to His great act of love. The evidence is that as human wickedness abounds, and suffering increases, He will still hold out to the very last possible moment before returning to end it all. This is because He wants as many as possible to share in the glories that shall be revealed. This new order will be perfect, brought into being by love. Truly, then, love will make "the world go 'round." Divine healing will then have run its course and have achieved its goal. What a miracle!

That lies in the future. We are men and women of today. The spiritually destitute, sick, infirm, possessed, bruised, and heartbroken are all around us.

The Bible gives us clear indication that, through the power of the Spirit, we need not await the Lord's return for them to be helped. Faith makes future blessings a *present* reality (Heb. 11:1). Already, by faith, we now have a foretaste of heavenly life; already, we can appropriate and apply Christ's victory over Satan in order to set the captives free. Even now, the sick can experience the healing power of Jesus. We have, therefore, an urgent and vital healing mission to the world of today. To the nature of that mission we must now turn.

PART THREE

RECEIVING AND MINISTERING SUPERNATURAL POWER

8

Commissioned to Heal

Jesus knew that He was destined to an early death. This was the divine master plan for the salvation of the human race. He also knew that He would rise again and return to the Father.

From very early in His ministry, therefore, He made preparations for His divine healing mission to be continued. He selected a small group of men, and began to train them for this vital work. These disciples were chosen to be the foundation members of what would become a vast society; they were the embryo of a new, living, growing organism—the Church. This new "race" and "nation of people" (1 Pet. 2:1-10)—from all nationalities (Rev. 5:9-10)—would continue every aspect of His work until His return in glory.

Jesus' ministry, therefore, was both extensive and intensive. On the one hand, He went out to teach and heal vast crowds of people, proclaiming to them the reality of the kingdom of God. On the other hand, He had long sessions alone with His disciples, giving them the intensive, specific training they needed in order eventually to carry on His work (Mark 4:10).

Jesus, however, was not content only to convey spiritual truths to these men, He was concerned that they should enter a very deep relationship with himself. For them to *know* Him was the secret of eternal life (John 17:3). He sought to share with them, therefore, the same union which He had with the Father, so that they also might tap the mainsprings of spiritual power (John 17).

When He felt that they were ready, "He called the twelve together and gave them power and authority over all demons and to cure diseases, and he sent them out to preach the kingdom of God and to heal. . . . And they departed and went through the villages, preaching the gospel and healing everywhere" (Luke 9:1-6).

The mission was such a success that Jesus sent out an even larger contingent of those He felt to be ready to mission. This time the number was seventy (Luke 10:1-24), with the command to enter cities and, "Heal the sick that are therein, and say unto them, The kingdom of God is come nigh unto you" (Luke 10:9 KJV). And the seventy returned with joy, saying "Lord, even the devils are subject unto us through thy name" (Luke 10:17 KJV).

At that time Jesus was filled with joy and thanked the Father that "All things have been delivered to me by my Father; and no one knows who the Son is except the Father, or who the Father is except the Son and any one to whom the Son chooses to reveal him" (Luke 10:22).

The significance of this prayer, in its context of successful mission, was that the source of healing power lay in a deep relationship with God, in Christ.

Both the mission of the twelve and that of the seventy

were, however, only training courses for the extensive task which the disciples were to undertake after Jesus had left them.

On the night before He was crucified He made an amazing prediction to His disciples, a prediction which contained a promise: "Truly, I say to you, he who believes in me will also do the works that I do; and greater works than these will he do, because I go to the Father" (John 14:12).

Soon after His resurrection, He also promised, "Ye shall be baptized with the Holy Ghost not many days hence. . . . Ye shall receive power, after that the Holy Ghost is come upon you: and ye shall be witnesses unto me both in Jerusalem, and in all Judaea, and Samaria, and unto the uttermost part of the earth" (Acts 1:5, 8 KJV).

It was on the feast of Pentecost, ten days after His ascension to heaven, that the promised power fell upon the first one hundred and twenty Christians. It came in an unmistakable way.

"And when the day of Pentecost was fully come, they were all with one accord in one place. And suddenly there came a sound from heaven as of a rushing mighty wind, and it filled all the house where they were sitting. And there appeared unto them cloven tongues like as of fire, and it sat upon each of them. And they were all filled with the Holy Ghost, and began to speak with other tongues, as the Spirit gave them utterance" (Acts 2:1-4 KJV).

Immediately they launched out upon their mission.

It is important to realize that in obedience to the Lord's command theirs was a "full" gospel, divine healing mission. They had a gospel for the whole person. Thus, their message was centered on the person of Jesus (Acts 2:22). It was, like His, fundamentally about the kingdom of God, which could be entered by an act of deep repentance (Acts 2:38). Thousands of spiritually destitute people responded to their message and were baptized (Acts 2:41).

Their ministry was also about healing of the body, and the record of their deeds goes into precise detail about their first miracle when they healed a man who had been lame since birth (Acts 3). After the miracle they pointed out to the crowds that the man had in fact been healed by the risen Jesus Christ on the grounds of his *faith* in Jesus' name (Acts 3:16). It is noteworthy also that the man had instantly *obeyed* the command, "In the Name of Jesus Christ of Nazareth rise up and walk" (Acts 3:6 KJV).

A large crowd had gathered at the news of this remarkable event. This gave Peter the chance to point from the sight of a healed man to the unseen reality of the risen Jesus. The result was that thousands more entered the kingdom of God.

In this, and subsequent healings, all the practices and principles of Jesus' own ministry were reproduced in the ministry of His disciples. Soon, as with Jesus, multitudes began to gather together. They came "from the towns around Jerusalem, bringing the sick and those afflicted with unclean spirits, and they were all healed" (Acts 5:16).

This ministry was not limited to the original apostles, but also involved those who heard about Jesus through their words. Already second generation Christians were discovering the same power as the apostles themselves as they obeyed the same command. One such believer was

Stephen, who is described as being "full of grace and power." He wrought "great wonders and signs among the people" (Acts 6:8).

Another such person was Stephen's fellow deacon, Philip. He went on a mission to the Samaritans, a race usually regarded by Jews as spiritual outcasts. These people, however, soon responded to the gospel, "And the multitudes with one accord gave heed to what was said by Philip, when they heard him and saw the signs which he did. For unclean spirits came out of many who were possessed, crying with a loud voice; and many who were paralyzed or lame were healed. So there was much joy in that city" (Acts 8:6-8).

The ministry of "release to the captives" was, therefore, continued in this and other missions of the early church.

It is significant that when Philip, and later Paul, met first-century occult supernaturalists, they in no way joined forces with them. On the contrary they rebuked them and sought to convert them. At least one, Simon the sorcerer, came to believe in the power of Jesus Christ (Acts 8:9-25).

The Christians of the early church fully understood Jesus' message and the full scope and methods of His ministry. They were people who, through the Holy Spirit, knew the experience of Jesus being always present with them (Acts 13:8-12).

Jesus' early command had been to "preach as you go. . . . Heal the sick, raise the dead, cleanse lepers, cast out demons" (Matt. 10:7-8).

They saw this work as an integrated whole, as different

aspects of one evangelistic task. For them, the ministry of healing the body was not an optional "extra." Neither was the casting out of demons a side issue to their main work. They continued the full *ministry* of Jesus, in the *power* of Jesus. There is not the remotest hint in the New Testament that the mission of the Church should be any other than the gospel of the kingdom for the healing of the whole person. The Acts of the Apostles gives adequate evidence that the first Christians were fully obedient to the command of their Lord.

The commission to supernatural ministry, therefore, rings forth loud and clear from the New Testament, the rule of belief and practice of the Christian Church in this and every age. From its pages we hear the call to divine healing and gospel mission to the crying needs of the world today.

It took me seventeen years, from my conversion in 1952 until my baptism in the Holy Spirit in 1969, to realize the full extent of the Church's mission. I had, of course, always understood that Christianity was about salvation, but I had been taught that this involved purely the salvation of the soul from sin and hell. It took visits to full gospel meetings in pentecostal churches to open my eyes and impel me to reread my Bible for the truth really to dawn. I saw then that Jesus had commissioned His Church with a gospel for the whole person—body, mind, and spirit—and that anything less was an inadequate concept of the gospel.

In 1970, I inaugurated a full gospel ministry in the parish church of St. Paul, Hainault. I saw God move in healing power in miracles of conversion, transformed lives, healing, and deliverance. It was these insights which eventually drove me beyond the confines of a parish church to an itinerant Power, Praise, and Healing Mission.

From the beginning I saw that such a mission had to be more than simply my arriving in an area to preach the gospel, heal the sick, and cast out demons. This would, of course, be good for all those saved and healed. But I saw that such a mission would be limited if I then left the churches of the area no further forward in their own full gospel ministry. I realized that a *good* mission would be when more happened after I had left than happened while I was there. My main aim in mission, therefore, has always been so to preach, teach, act, and minister that the local church would feel impelled and inspired to go on with the work of full gospel mission. This I felt to be a *dynamic*, rather than *static*, concept of the work of a healing evangelist—the only approach to mission which was of relevance to the crying needs of the world today.

For this to happen, a first priority was to convince local leaders that they could not avoid the implication of Christ's commission to the church in their area. I had to show them that as the manifestation of the body of Christ, the flesh and blood media through which He ministers today in each locality, they had to take up the challenge of the gospel for the whole person. I had to show them that they had no option but to launch out to obey our Lord's command: "Preach the gospel, heal the sick and cast out demons."

For this reason, I have never undertaken a mission without inviting the local church leaders to minister with me. What joy it has brought me to see men of God renewed in their ministries in this way, as they have stood side by side with me, in front of their often amazed people, and seen the sick wonderfully healed!

I have, in fact, seen these aftereffects in nearly every mission I have taken. These are typical letters:

"I ought to have written to you long before this to say how much I was personally blessed as a result of your brief tent mission in Cheadle. My ministry has been blessed and my life enriched." (Methodist minister)

"I wish I could find words to describe the joy that has hit our church over the last few days. The God of wonders has poured out so many blessings we want to just praise Him and praise Him. One lady came to the church for the first time on Sunday night. She was healed and gloriously saved. She surprised the lady in the post office when she went to collect her Social Security money. She had not been able to walk for weeks and weeks. She is encouraging lots of people to come to our own new Power, Praise, and Healing meetings next Sunday evening. We feel sure that the mission last weekend was only a *beginning* and we are continuing to have exactly the same services every Sunday night." (Church of England vicar, Brighton)

"I believe that your visit has given us a new start with a new vision and purpose. I have had reports of healing and have been asked for the laying on of hands by some people who missed you. I have used the ministry before but now there is a difference." (Church of England vicar, North Midlands)

He went on to list the healing of a lady in severe pain with a trapped nerve, another suffering from acute insomnia, and a lady suffering from ulcerative colitis and a liver condition.

"The overall effect of the mission has been very deep. It has made a very great impression upon the residents of this parish. We are much in prayer that the effect of the mission will lead many to minister power, praise, and healing in this area, and that we ourselves might fulfill our Lord's command to heal the sick and preach the Word to those in such darkness around us." (Church of England vicar, Central London)

Actually this parish, where previously only a few people ever went to church, experienced such a move of God's Spirit that now they have a regular full gospel ministry, where blessing continually abounds in a desperately needy area of London. A spiritual wilderness has at least one oasis!

Such letters indicate that the dynamic vision of mission with which I began my itinerant work in 1975 has already been more than fulfilled.

9

Supernaturally Endowed

It is interesting that in one of the letters I quoted, the vicar wrote, "I have used the ministry before, but now there is a difference."

Why was this? I believe it is because during our mission this vicar, like hundreds of church leaders I have known, became supernaturally endowed for his ministry with the Holy Spirit's gifts of healing (1 Cor. 12:9, 28).

The gospels record that even Jesus himself had to receive "power from on high" before He could begin His divine healing mission.

"Now, when all the people were baptized, it came to pass, that Jesus also being baptized, and praying, the heaven was opened, And the Holy Ghost descended in a bodily shape like a dove . . ." (Luke 3:21-22 KJV).

"And Jesus being full of the Holy Ghost returned from Jordan" (Luke 4:1 KJV).

The disciples had to receive a similar endowment before they could begin their supernatural ministry (Acts 1:5,24).

The same is obviously true for ministers of healing

today. Yet, at the time of my ordination to Holy Orders, the Church of England taught me nothing at all about moving powerfully in the realm of the supernatural. It had, for centuries, stood for dignified, respectable, safe Christianity. Although both its "Catholic" and "Evangelical" wings had a definite spirituality and sought, in their different ways, to communicate the grace of God to the faithful, supernatural phenomena were not really in evidence and the concept of the miraculous was regarded as a matter of early church history.

Consequently, until 1969, my own ministry was very ordinary. Although I had worked hard as a pastor, I eventually became so disillusioned and frustrated that I forsook full-time parish ministry for a post in religious education.

It was, in fact, the pentecostal branch of the Christian Church, whose supernatural emphasis had for so long been rejected by major denominations, which awakened stirrings in my soul for an endowment of supernatural power. It was what I witnessed in their full gospel meetings that first made me realize the possibilities of ministering God's power today. Hadn't the natural life of mankind been completely revolutionized by new discoveries of physical power? I reasoned, "How much more could happen to our spiritual lives through the rediscovery of spiritual power?"

Coal, gas, electricity, oil and, more recently, nuclear power have transformed our lives. Yet these vast resources of physical energy had existed for countless generations, while human beings had labored in their own strength to achieve their objectives. It had been the *realization* of these resources of power which had been the first step towards the accomplishments of modern technology.

The trouble with the Church, I decided, was that it had labored on without realizing the vast resources of spiritual power God had placed at its disposal since the first Pentecost. The pentecostal churches had helped me to realize that this endowment of the Spirit had not simply been for Peter, James, John, Mary, and the others, but a gift for the whole *Church*, for all time. It had dawned upon me that all the power of heaven was available to us today.

I remembered that although the first apostles had been very ordinary people like ourselves, the Acts of the Apostles told the thrilling story of what they had accomplished when the Spirit of God had come upon them. It was, I decided, my intensive schooling in rationalism which had caused me to lose my expectancy of what God could do today. Like myself, the few people who still attended church went expecting only the same unexciting routines week by week. The service would always take the same form and last approximately the same time. Before going to worship they could even put meat in the oven and set it ready for lunchtime. Everything was so mundane and so predictable.

We were so accustomed to the ordinary and so used to plodding on in our own strength that we had become conditioned to God's activity being a non-event. We were like the Arabs who, years ago, regularly struggled across the desert without realizing that under their feet were oceans of oil that could drive tons of metal across those same deserts at tremendous speed. Similarly, we

Christians had had incredible spiritual power 'above' us for nearly two thousand years, but had never realized its potential. The full meaning of Paul's words, "Now unto him that is able to do exceeding abundantly above all that we ask or think, according to the power that worketh in us" (Eph. 3:20 KJV), had never really been grasped by the church of my generation.

I can hardly exaggerate the effect this realization had upon me. It caused me to enter into a new dimension of spiritual power. I am sure that since that time one of the beneficial results of services like my Power, Praise and Healing meetings has been that they awakened the realization that the supernatural power of the Spirit is still available for Christians today.

A second important principle relating to power, however, is that once its possibilities have been released, it still has to be brought within our grasp in order to be useful. Oil, for instance, is no use under the North Sea; it has to be brought ashore in order to be productive. Coal is no use under the earth; miners have to bring it to the surface before it can be used. Similarly, once we have realized the resource of power we have today in the Holy Spirit we must lay hold of it—receive it—in order to use it for a spiritual revolution. Paul asked some men of Ephesus, "have ye received the Holy Ghost since ye believed?" (Acts 19:2 KJV). And this is still a pertinent question for Christians today. Before 1969, I, like those Ephesians, would have had to answer, "I do not know the Holy Spirit is given."

Providentially, receiving the power of the Holy Spirit is a great deal easier than getting oil from the North Sea, for

God is more ready to give than we are to receive (Matt. 21:22). Jesus said, "How much more shall your heavenly Father give the Holy Spirit to them that ask Him?" (Luke 11:13 KJV).

Receiving the power of the Holy Spirit is not so much, therefore, a matter of intensive effort, but of getting our lives into the right relationship with God. It is more like refueling a car or plane than digging for coal. To put more gas into a car, we have to bring it into right alignment with the pump at the service station. Similarly, a small fighter plane has to be brought into exactly the right "relationship" with the "parent" plane in order to refuel in midair. When receiving the Holy Spirit, *a right personal relationship with God* is essential.

Occultists look in all directions for sources of supernatural power. Sometimes, without realizing it, they refuel at a service station provided by the devil. The gift of the *Holy* Spirit, however, is for children of the kingdom whose lives have been brought into a right relationship with God through repentance and acceptance of Christ as Savior. Then the gift of the power of the Spirit is available by an act of simple faith. The biblical prescription is, "Repent, and be baptized every one of you in the name of Jesus Christ for the remission of sins, and ye shall receive the gift of the Holy Ghost. For the promise is unto you, and to your children, and to all that are afar off, even as many as the Lord our God shall call" (Acts 2: 38-39 KJV).

Typically, many Christians can be likened to a man laboring in a faraway country. He finds the work hard and the hours long. He earns little money. One day, however, a visitor recognizes him.

"Don't you know," he says, "that back home your rich brother has died and left you an immense fortune?"

The poor laborer can hardly believe it!

"How long ago did it happen?" he asks.

"Why, about twenty years ago" is the reply.

The poor fellow realizes that he has been living like a pauper, when all the time he has, in fact, been a millionaire. He catches the next plane home, goes to the bank, presents evidence of his identity, and begins to draw upon his wealth.

That was how it was with me when a pentecostal evangelist showed me the fullness of my inheritance as a child of God (Rom. 8:16). Once the realization of my position had dawned I wasted no time in going to the bank of heaven in order to receive my inheritance. I knew that my life was right with God through my faith in the crucified and risen Christ. I was a child of the kingdom. I now knew that I could receive the promise of the Holy Spirit. I immediately asked for the laying on of hands, the usual channel by which the power is communicated. I experienced the evidence of the promised infilling on May 28, 1969, in the quietness of my own home in Harlow, Essex. I was on my knees praising the Lord, when I seemed to run out of ordinary words. I was caught up in unutterable joy. I let my tongue loose and began to speak in a manner which I realized must be the gift of tongues mentioned in the Acts of the Apostles (Acts 2:1-12). I was literally lost in rapture, ecstasy and bliss. It seemed I was being lifted up to heaven, blessed, blessed, and blessed again. For nearly two hours this language flowed from my mouth as I praised the Lord in this new, wonderful language.

Spiritual experiences are difficult to describe but I felt a release, ecstasy, and new power, all at the same time. I knew I had been supernaturally endowed for a supernatural ministry. I had at last broken through into new realms of power.

Studies in the Acts of the Apostles had led me to see, however, that insight into another form of power was necessary before I could really be an effective minister of divine healing. Once again the modern world helped me to understand just what it was.

We think of power today not only in the terms of "energy," but also in those of "politics." After an election, or a coup d'état, we say that a new administration has come into power. By this we mean that some person or group of people has been given, or has taken, authority to rule. Unless they are to be accounted traitors or rebels their subjects must acknowledge their rule and obey their laws.

Christians, in fact, belong to two kingdoms at once—the earthly and the heavenly. They respect and obey their earthly rulers (though not always without question), and also (definitely without question) subscribe to the ultimate authority of their Lord, Jesus Christ. Christians have often been martyred because of this undeniable allegiance to the ultimate authority of the Lord Jesus Christ over their lives.

Jesus, in fact, first portrayed His unique authority during His ministry in first-century Palestine. It was His remarkable authority in teaching, dealing with demons, sickness, circumstances, the forces of nature, and even death, which drew gasps of astonishment from the crowds. Ultimately, His authority was gloriously demonstrated when He rose from the dead. After this remarkable event He declared to His disciples, "All authority in heaven and on earth has been given to me" (Matt. 28:18).

Christians are those who have submitted to the authority and lordship of Jesus, the "King of kings."

Authority, however, is often delegated to subordinates. By this means, rulers trust and enable others to implement their wishes. So, an "officer of the Crown" may be a very insignificant and unimportant man in normal life, but he is conscious of a very important role indeed when carrying out the instructions of his government. The power he yields has been delegated to him from above. It is effective as long as he remains obedient and faithful in his tasks.

It is wonderfully true also that Jesus, the King of kings, has delegated to *His* subordinates, the children of the kingdom, His unique and wonderful spiritual authority. He has done this by giving us the right to use *His name* as we obey His commission to preach the gospel, heal the sick and cast out demons. We Christians can receive the *energy*-power of heaven and exercise the *authority*-power of the King of kings. What immense, incalculable resources we have at our disposal for the transformation of human life!

Once again we see the vital difference between divine healing and mere supernaturalism. Divine healing is ministered through a power which emanates from Jesus and by an authority vested in the use of *His* name. His name guarantees His personal presence, power, authority, and effectiveness, for all who know Him, trust Him, acknowledge His position, and obey His commands.

In my missioning I have found it vitally necessary to share these insights about power and authority with pastors and people whom I have been urging to fulfill our Lord's commission to preach the gospel, heal the sick, and cast out demons; otherwise, the result would only have been despair, disillusionment, and failure. When, however, Christians have truly received the power and used their authority, they have seen glory in the church.

Apathy, complacency, and spiritual self-satisfaction are the main enemies of revival. We need both a dynamic concept of *mission* and also a dynamic concept of *life in the power of the Holy Spirit* in order to move effectively in God's will. More and more power is ours as we seek Him at greater and greater depths, increasingly submitting to His promptings, and courageously launching out in obedience to His commands. Our resolution should increasingly be (in Hudson Taylor's words) to "Expect great things *from* God and attempt great things *for* God."

Our prayer should be:
"Let the fire fall, let the fire fall
Floods of revival; Lord, let them fall
Streams of salvation reaching to all.

Open the windows of heaven we pray
. . . O for a deluge of Holy Ghost power
Lord, we are waiting, send it this hour."

"Spirit of the living God,
Fall afresh on me.
Spirit of the living God, fall afresh on me.
Break me, melt me, mold me, fill me,
Spirit of the living God, fall afresh on me."

Time after time, God has answered this prayer at my meetings. I have seen tremendous, indescribable, heavenly visitations with scores of people falling to the earth, praising, worshiping, and prophesying as God has endowed them with "manifold gifts of the Holy Spirit."

Many pastors have received gifts of healing as I have prayed over them and then ministered to the sick. Others have actually received the power *as they have begun* to minister to them. The evidence of their being used in this ministry has not been simply that people have fallen to the ground, but, much more important, that people have actually been healed through the laying on of their hands.

At the end of some meetings, I have seen whole churches receive supernatural anointing in a moment of time. I have heard hundreds of people begin to cry out with joy as the Spirit has come upon them.

After my visit to Singapore, Canon Frank Lomax, vicar of the island's St. Andrew's Cathedral, wrote in *Network*, the United Society for the Propagation of the Gospel mission newspaper, January 1976:

Christians old and new standing shoulder to shoulder in the Cathedral sanctuary and aisles sung in uninhibited joy—some in tongues—all with a new experience of the Spirit's infilling, with a new awareness of the living God and Father.

On the last night of the Mission—a stranger wandering through the Cathedral grounds was drawn by the sound of singing and looked in through the west door. He later described what he saw:

"The whole sanctuary was ablaze with fire. I closed my eyes in unbelief and opened them again. Flames of fire filled the whole East end. . . ."

It certainly described in visual form what was happening to those of us who were standing in the Lord's house.

The gifts received and ministries granted on such occasions have of course been manifested after the mission. Many of the results we shall, perhaps, never hear about this side of eternity. Letters, however, regularly arrive at my office giving constant testimony to the fact that God has visited His people, revitalizing and equipping them for supernatural ministry by the bestowal of power and authority. (See Acts 2:1-4.)

10

Using the Gift

When I began to challenge pastors to launch out into Spirit-empowered ministry, I was soon brought to realize that such men feel very insecure when they find themselves to be getting out of their depth. Most reacted favorably to suggestions about "preaching the gospel" because that was what they had generally been trained to do. It was a different matter, however, when I came to the need to lay hands on the sick. Such teaching often met with real hostility. Frequently, when talking to groups of ministers, I discovered that underlying their objections to this ministry was the fact that they did not know just when, where, or how to begin. I have had every sympathy with them in their dilemma, because some years ago I had exactly the same problem—I had no idea how to minister to sick people or even what results to expect.

Most ministers, of course, are very ready to pray for the sick in their absence because this has been the accepted procedure in the tradition of most denominations of the church. As a pastor I had done so myself, nearly every Sunday, even to mentioning the needy people by name. Many ministers, I discovered, had even gone as far as praying in the *presence* of sick people, when visiting them in their homes. Such prayers had, of course, always included an "if it be thy will" clause. These words sound pious enough, but they cut at the very root of faith as "taking it for granted that we are actually receiving that which we ask." They can be simply a way of escape in case nothing happens. Such prayers demand little faith of either church or pastor.

In pastors' gatherings, however, I have refused to accept these practices as a complete ministry to the sick. I have pointed to the example of our Lord, and indeed to the whole New Testament, as showing clearly that the Bible not only tells about praying for the sick in their *absence*, but of *ministering* to them in their *presence*. Of course, I have readily acknowledged that God does answer intercessory prayer for the sick—because He is an all-powerful, faithful, loving Father. However, that is not the way into supernatural power and the realm of healing miracles. Actually, *to minister* to the sick, as did Jesus and the early Christians, had proved for me to be a breakthrough into the supernatural dimension in healing. I had seen it to be so in the ministries of scores of others. Ever since, therefore, I have urged it as the way of obedience for every pastor I have met.

The firm line I have taken has definite support from the Epistle of James. Addressing sick Christians, apparently too ill to be "at church," the inspired writer urges:

Is any sick among you? let him call for the elders of the church; and let them pray over him, anointing

him with oil in the name of the Lord: And the prayer
of faith shall save the sick, and the Lord shall raise
him up; and if he have committed sins, they shall be
forgiven him. Confess your faults one to another, and
pray for one another, that ye may be healed. The
effectual fervent prayer of a righteous man availeth
much. (James 5:14-16 KJV)

This passage is very interesting because it teaches:

(a) The elders of the church are to minister, as *elders*.
There is no suggestion that they are especially gifted.
They are certainly not visiting evangelists on a special
healing mission. The fact that James says that the *elders*
are to minister shows that healing ministry is envisaged
as part of the supernaturally *normal* life of the church.

(b) They actually *minister* to the sick person as Jesus
did, using words, hands, and even oil. There is no
suggestion that praying for this person in his absence
should be the normal procedure. Quite the opposite is
true. James urges that when a Christian is sick, he should
call for the elders. On receiving this request, their duty is
not simply to pray for the sick person at the next church
service, but *to go and minister directly to his needs*.

(c) Faith is seen as a very important factor in healing.
There is no questioning of God's will. Healing, whether
sudden or gradual, is normative and is to be taken for
granted. It is the result to be expected. This is in harmony
with the teaching of the Lord of the church about the
nature of faith.

(d) The character of the ministers is implied. They are
righteous in their character and also men of faithful,

powerful prayer.

(e) We see, as in the ministry of our Lord, that forgiveness of sin and the healing of the body are very closely linked. Apparently unconfessed sin, is, like doubt, a barrier to healing. Again, we see that the healing of the soul is basic to the health of the body. This is where the emphasis of James's ministry is squarely placed. Confession is good for the soul, for the body, and for the whole person.

This passage shows us, I believe, the normal procedure in dealing with sickness in the early church. This was how the early Christians were taught, and, no doubt, this was how they acted. There is not the slightest reason for abandoning this practice today.

This ministry of elders, however, presupposes the existence of a church which itself is healthy, united, expectant, and powerful. This is because the elders are not using their own gift, but are ministering the endowment which God has bestowed upon *the Church*. Theirs is a representative act, performed on behalf of the whole church to which they belong.

The reason for this is better understood if we turn to Paul's first letter to the church at Corinth. There, as in other places, he teaches that the church is like a body which has many "members" or, as we would say, "organs" (1 Cor. 12, Rom. 12, Eph. 4). The important factor about parts of our bodies is that they share a common life, energy, and health. They are all served by the same bloodstream and are dependent upon each other for their very life. If a part of the body, for instance, the kidney, becomes sick, then the whole body is vitally affected. "If one member suffers, all suffer together" (1 Cor. 12:26).

In fact, from modern medical knowledge, we can go further than Paul, and say here positively, "If one member (organ) is sick, all the healing power of the body rushes to its aid."

All the healing resources of the body unite to overcome the threat to its life.

Here we have a picture of the church's (eldership) ministry of healing. A "member" of the church "body" becomes sick. Therefore, all the other members, the rest of the church, feel his pain. The whole church is involved. The elders, therefore, are called to lay hands on the sick person. In doing so, they function as the vital organs of the whole body. They are the channels through which the healing power of the body will flow to the sick member. However, the health of the *whole* body is involved—not just that of the elders themselves. The elders call upon all the faith, prayer, and love resources of the church to be behind them in their ministry. If there is disunity, discord, and doubt prevalent in the body, the flow of God's healing Spirit will be impeded.

It was a sad fact that the church of Corinth was itself sinfully divided. Paul had to write, "For this cause many are weak and sickly among you, and many sleep" (1 Cor. 11:30 KJV).

Healing ministry was apparently not effective at Corinth, a church that excelled in supernatural gifts, because they brought their sinful self-love even to the Communion service and did not "discern the Lord's body" (v. 29).

Today's healing ministry, unfortunately, can

sometimes be caricatured as a congregation coming together like a crowd who have turned up to watch spectacular events. They have no sense of being a body of believers or of having a vital part to play in the ministry. "Let's go to see if it works"; "Let's see if the pastor can heal someone this week!" "He's not doing very well—probably because he's out of tune with the Lord" are the unspoken thoughts of many people.

The pastor, therefore, feels himself to be "out on his own." Even if, as he should, he calls the other elders to join him in ministering, they too can begin to feel that, humanly speaking, healing depends entirely upon them.

"We have not been able to heal many people," they may conclude. "We had better send for an evangelist to see if he can do better!"

I have often been conscious that this has been the attitude of large parts of the congregation at so-called "Miracle Services." People can so easily have come along to watch some spiritual performer "do his stuff." When I have sensed the prevalence of this attitude, I have stopped ministering and explained to the Christians that we are all involved together in the work. I have called them to earnest, expectant prayer. We have then praised the Lord together for those who are healed.

Very occasionally it may be right that the emphasis is mainly on the gifts of a very special person, but even then that person needs enormous prayer support. These times are, however, exceptions to the general rule. I believe that the Lord's *primary* purpose today is to restore all over the world the *Church's* ministry of healing for the good of His people and the extension of His kingdom.

This is so despite the fact that throughout history, God has raised up specifically gifted people and focused attention upon them. He has done so also in our time. This has been, however, for the inspiration and encouragement of the whole Church. Christians totally misunderstand the purposes of God if they see such gifted ministries as superseding or replacing the regular ministries of the church. The work of especially gifted people, in any sphere of ministry, is not to draw attention to themselves. It is their function to *encourage*, inspire, teach, and further the normal ministry, which should be in progress everywhere because Christ is present in *His Church*.

In this respect we can draw a parallel between the role of the the gifted healer and that of the gifted preacher. It is customary for a sermon to be preached in every Christian church on the Lord's Day. The eldership of the local church has an obligation to see that this is so, either by doing so themselves, or by appointing someone else to preach. They do not wait for one of the world's gifted preachers to arrive before someone goes into the pulpit! The church has a duty to preach regularly! If a gifted preacher arrives, he may well be given prominence and inspire the church—but the local preaching does not depend on such. It goes on all the time! It is exactly the same with the healing ministry and "gifted" healers. Every church, everywhere, should minister to the sick as part of its normal church life; when gifted healers arrive, it is to inspire and encourage the regular healing ministry of the church.

Eldership is conceived of differently by different

denominations, but it is always present, because the church could not function without it. In most denominations the "ordained" ministers or "clergy" are the focal point of eldership, but their office is not exclusive. When I was a vicar, my churchwardens ministered with me, as elders. Baptists and other denominations have "deacons" to take this role. Presbyterians certainly have lay elders. There is no excuse for not getting on with the job.

Special people are, therefore, by no means essential for the healing ministry. Neither does healing ministry need special times or places. The proper *place* for healing ministry is either "on the spot" where the sick person actually is, or where the church body regularly meets for worship. The *time* similarly should either be that which is spontaneously provided by the Lord, or the regular and normal time believers meet together for ministry and worship. I have deliberately stayed in churches where I have been missioning in order to minister to the needs of the people during normal Sunday services. Sometimes this has been in the content of a Communion service, during the partaking of the bread and wine; on other occasions it has been during the prayer time in morning or evening worship. Another suitable moment has been during the hymn after the sermon, thus enabling the request for ministry to be in response to the spoken word. In some cases ministry has taken place in an "after-meeting" for which, in my experience, most people have willingly stayed.

I have found that special prayer groups for the sick, perhaps midweek, in a home, hall, or vestry, have sometimes been necessary as an intermediary stage in introducing divine healing ministry to a church or area. The aim, however, must eventually be to have the gospel of the healing of the whole person proclaimed by words and deeds when the whole body of believers usually meets for worship.

If the ministry is to be seen in its evangelistic as well as its pastoral perspective, it is also important that everyone in the locality is made aware that healing ministry is practiced in their local church. They must feel free to come, and know when this ministry is available. It is for this reason that regularity of ministry, at the customary services, is a distinct advantage. We have really "arrived" when divine healing ministry is as normal as receiving Communion or hearing a sermon. Expectancy, however, must always be encouraged.

Like all other aspects of church life, divine healing ministry can be "inaugurated" or "boosted" by having a time of special emphasis upon it. This can be a time for inviting a gifted guest minister along to help the local church. Mass leaflet distribution, posters, media coverage, and personal testimonies can be brought into play. I have often taken part in such efforts at the invitation of churches and the results have truly glorified the Lord as we have seen hundreds of people who would normally be considered "outsiders" converted to Christ.

The fact is that most people search for God to meet the needs of their bodies, minds, or circumstances before they ever understand the importance of the salvation of their souls. It was mainly physical needs which brought people seeking the help of Christ and the apostles. It is the same today with His Church.

It is important that people are not compelled to become "disciples" *before* their physical needs are met. This was never so with Jesus. In the case of the ten lepers, sadly, only one even bothered to come back to give thanks. Similarly, we must minister today to all who come to us sincerely. However, we also remember that our Lord's ministry to physical needs was always against the background of the proclamation of the kingdom of God. There must, in our day, therefore, be no separation of the healing of the body or mind from the total message of the reign of Christ over the whole of human life.

11

Rites and Ceremonies

Divine healing has been much neglected by the Church, and very few pastors have received training in ministry to the sick. Yet, as we have seen, this ministry is not an optional extra, but an essential part of the gospel. It should, therefore, regularly be presented in every church of every denomination. It is to be hoped that those responsible for training ministers for work in the world today will see the urgency of this matter and not send out into Christian service men and women who are ill-prepared for this vital task.

It is interesting to note that in the current spate of liturgical revision which is taking place in most denominations, divine healing has been sadly neglected. In the Church of England no order of service has been presented for ratification since the 1662 "Visitation of the Sick." This particular order is strong in its emphasis on repentance, but needs drastic revision in the light of new insight into the teaching of the Bible on this subject. The Roman Catholic Sacrament of Extreme Unction is, in fact, a survival of the ministry of anointing the sick with oil found in the book of James. Yet, for many centuries it has been linked here with preparation for death rather than with expectation of healing. There are signs that this attitude is changing (I understand that recent instructions about using this service permit it for less extreme illnesses than before) but a great deal of work still needs to be done before a real healing ministry is explicit in the act.

Pentecostal denominations also can hardly escape criticism in this respect. The ethos of their worship and ministry is, of course, nonliturgical. However, in leaving matters entirely to the "leading of the Spirit" there has been a tendency for young pastors simply to imitate others. Also, because of lack of teaching about the corporate aspect of this ministry—that it involves the whole church—some have given up ministering to the sick in despair, while others have never actually started for fear of failure.

For most church leaders, therefore, some order of service would be a real help as they begin to minister to the sick. It would also give their congregations both confidence and insight into this vital work. Some definite guidelines are needed. We must beware, however, of lapsing into a "magical" use of correct rituals or such a formal approach that expectancy is lost. Most recent liturgies for other services have maintained a healthy balance between the need for order and leaving room for spontaneity. I have found both to be important in this ministry. While acknowledging our human fallibility and need for guidance, we need also to emulate the freedom with which Jesus himself approached every separate case of sickness. Orders of service must give plenty of scope for the discernment of the ultimate source of the symptoms and variety of method in the application of the healing power.

Because I had received no training in this field I began as inexperienced as anyone could be. Visits to pentecostal churches had made me realize the possibilities of this ministry and had set me seeking the assurance of the supernatural endowment I felt I desperately needed to minister in the realm of the miraculous. I had also seen in pentecostalism a pattern of ministry I could copy. When in 1970 I became vicar of St. Paul's Church, Hainault, I was further challenged to begin divine healing ministry by the churchwardens specifically asking me to do so. I did not feel at all certain, however, how I would minister in an Anglican situation and I was very sure that a pentecostal approach would be too far removed from the worshiping tradition of the people to be acceptable.

I had heard that an Anglican clergyman, Rev. Roy Jeremiah of the London Healing Mission had once visited St. Paul's to teach about divine healing and so I decided to go to his church and see how he actually did it! I noted there that the laying on of hands was the focal point in the worship, and that it was performed while people knelt reverently at the altar rail. From this position they whispered their need, or the need of an absent friend, to the minister, who prayed quietly, spontaneously, and appropriately over them. The prayer was gentle, firm, and definite. The whole service proceeded with joy, expectancy, and yet with dignity. I was much impressed and began a monthly service like that in my own church.

My first congregation numbered only twelve people, but I felt that the Lord was truly blessing us. The service always moved in the following way:

Act of worship—hymns and prayers

Corporate act of confession and claiming of the promises of Christ's forgiving Word

Bible reading and exposition—with a theme related to healing

Hymn and prayer claiming the presence and power of the Holy Spirit

Period of silent prayer and preparation

Act of laying on of hands, as at the London Healing Mission, while the congregation sang hymns and prayed with me for each person

Thanksgiving for all God had done

Closing act of worship

Blessing

The service was conducted around the holy table, with our two candles lit and myself fully robed.

It was some months after the introduction of this service that my pentecostal friends asked me to take a meeting in their church, which would include ministry to the sick. Although I agreed to go, I was even more nervous about the prospect of this new venture than the one at St. Paul's. I was not used to conducting penetecostal meetings and felt I might not be able to handle the situation. How would I, an Anglican parson, fit into their free, spontaneous ethos? My wife and ten other people from St. Paul's, Hainault, accepted my invitation to be with me for the occasion. I had decided that I would ask the pastor actually to minister to the sick, while I watched to see if there was anything I could learn from his experienced ministry.

The evening did not go at all as I had planned! After I had preached and called sick people to stand at the front of the church, I realized, to my horror, that the pastor was quite definitely going to leave it all to me. There was no escape! I placed my hands on the head of the first person and, to my amazement, in this atmosphere of free, uninhibited worship, I suddenly felt a new freedom and surge of power. Words, both in English and other tongues poured from my lips, and the anointing of the Spirit was so great that person after person fell to the floor from under my hands.

Twenty-four-year-old Carol, who had come to the meeting from Hainault, was undergoing a terrible nervous breakdown. She looked more like a woman of forty as she stood in the healing line. She later described her experience at the meeting to a newspaper reporter:

My marriage broke up nearly three years ago and I took it very bad. I spent some time in a psychiatric hospital. I returned home dependent on anti-depressant tablets and sleeping pills.

I used to hide in my room and chain smoke all day. My mother told Mr. Dearing about the state I was in and he persuaded me to come along.

I can't remember doing it, but I went forward. Mr. Dearing laid hands on me and prayed for me.

When I walked out of the church I found the nearest drain and threw my tablets down it. I realized God loved me and had healed me.

Carol said, "Prayer saved my sanity." According to Jesus' terminology, she had been suffering from a broken heart.

She has since qualified as a nurse in a psychiatric hospital and has the matron's award as "nurse of the year."

Kate, a middle-aged housewife from Hainault, had a different, yet even more wonderful, experience at that pentecostal church meeting. All her life she had been a sincere, yet formal, worshiper and believer, first in her native Scotland, and then, from the time of the Second World War, in London.

As the service drew to a close, deeply moved by all she had seen and heard, she felt impelled to acknowledge her need of Jesus as her Savior and Lord. She came running forward in tears. I prayed over her and she really came to *know* the Jesus whom she had served for so long.

From that time I realized that my own ministry had to have much more the ingredients of freedom, spontaneity, expectancy, and joy. I had to operate within an evangelistic as well as a sacramental ethos.

Our Tuesday evening meetings at St. Paul's, therefore, began more and more to take on this atmosphere. Soon, crowds began to gather and hundreds began to be converted, as well as healed. Eventually, the needs of people abounded so much that I had to make the meetings weekly. However, I have by no means abandoned the lessons I had learned in the early days of my ministry. I still frequently minister within a more sacramental, "body," "eldership" context within the normal services of the church, as well as in the "charismatic," "gifted," evangelistic ethos. The Lord heals through both.

Obviously, however, as my function these days is mainly evangelistic, reaching those outside, as well as within the church, my emphasis is more on the free, pentecostal approach, which presupposes no liturgical tradition on the part of the hearers. I do, however, wherever the opportunity arises, minister fully robed, within the ethos of the more formal sacramental or other eldership tradition of the church. At such times appropriate prayers have been said, like these:

"In obedience to our Lord's command I lay upon you the healing hands of the Holy Spirit. May you be restored to fullness of health and strength, in body, mind, and spirit, so that you may serve the Lord faithfully, in the fellowship of His Church." Or, "May the Spirit of the risen Christ, who is with us now, enter your spirit, soul, mind, and body, driving away from you all that hurts you, and fill you with His peace."

Generally speaking, I have reserved the use of oil for these services, which have been outside the usual open-ended invitation of an evangelistic mission. I have felt that the use of consecrated oil, a biblical symbol for the healing power and presence of the Holy Spirit, should, like Holy Communion, be only for committed Christians. When appropriate, I have dipped my forefinger in oil and made the sign of the cross on the forehead. I have, however, used a liberal amount, and not been dismayed to see it gently trickling down a person's face. I have also agreed with Roman Catholics that the use of oil is particularly appropriate in cases of extreme sickness. For this reason, in church, hospital or home, whatever the form of service, I have always had a cruse of oil near to hand.

I remember one occasion when the use of oil was particularly precious to a person. This was in the case of Marcia, a pretty, clergyman's wife with four children. She had been deeply depressed after the birth of her fourth child and her depression became darker every day.

She sobbed through the first two hours of an evangelistic-type service which I was conducting. She was due to see her psychiatrist the next day and knew that, humanly speaking, a fourth admittance into a mental hospital was inevitable.

Her illness was so acute that she had to take massive doses of tranquilizers and sedatives, but life was still intolerable.

Marcia was too distressed to move out of her pew to receive ministry, so I laid hands on her as she sat in the choir stalls. After the prayer she became peaceful and I felt particularly led to ask her to come forward to receive a further ministry, that of anointing with oil.

She said afterwards that as she felt the oil running down her face it helped her to drink in more and more of the power of the Holy Spirit. She emerged from the ministry a transformed woman.

The psychiatrist was amazed at the remarkable change in his patient, who was now filled with joy and happiness. She was immediately able to manage without her tablets. A month later the psychiatrist saw her again and found her able to look after her family and support her husband's ministry with confidence.

Another occasion where I felt ministry with oil to be appropriate was in the case of a lady who had suffered severe injuries as the result of a car accident. I visited her home at the request of her doctor and found her to be paralyzed. I knew her to be a Christian, and, therefore, asked her if she would like to be anointed with oil. When she indicated that this was her desire, I stood over her bed, praying and putting oil liberally on her body. Her doctor later stated: "There was a dramatic change in her condition after she saw Rev. Dearing. She can now walk unaided and her internal injuries—which medical treatment could not help further—are now cured. There is no doubt in my mind that the Rev. Dearing was responsible for her recovery."

Although oil was used on both these and hundreds of other occasions, no fixed prayers were in fact used. I believe the results would have been the same, however, in any case. These people responded to the Lord, in faith, love, and obedience. The oil was simply but effectively a material help to their appropriating His power.

We can see from the New Testament that the work of the Church, like that of its Master, has two main aspects—the extensive ministry to the crowds (evangelism), and the intensive ministry to its own people (teaching). This distinction has always been implicit in its life and worship, where Holy Communion including the teaching of the faith has been the privilege of the committed and gospel services and missions a proclamation to the outsider. I believe that, in general, this distinction also applies to the healing ministry. There is an evangelistic, free, spontaneous ministry of laying on of hands based on a proclamation of the gospel message when "whosoever will may come." This was the ministry I discovered at the pentecostal church. There is also a close, interior, "body ministry," including teaching, for the committed, that which I first saw at the London Healing Mission. This is within the context of worship at depth and is an expression of pastoral care and mutual love. It is more definitely liturgical, drawing on the rich traditions of the church. Holiness is its theme and the laying on of hands is complemented by the use of oil.

As in all other aspects of the faith, however, every local church situation has an obligation to fulfill both tasks. Proclamation and teaching, order and freedom, spontaneity and the use of proven forms, penitence, love, joy, thanksgiving, dedication, and obedience must all have their part as the Lord moves *in* His Church to heal its sick and *through* His Church to reach the needy world outside. "Preach the gospel, heal the sick, cast out demons" is an irrevocable obligation wherever Christ is named as Lord. It is the activity of the *whole* Church.

12

Healing Hands

"I wish that *His* hands
Had been placed on *my* head
That *His* arms had been thrown around *me*."

This children's hymn surely expresses the longing of all Christians because it was the touch of Jesus which transformed sickness into health. This beautiful devotional thought is also contained in a lovely song, so often used in healing services today:

"He touched me, O, He touched me,
And, O, the joy that floods my soul;
Something happened and now I know
He touched me and made me whole."

But Jesus can no longer *physically* touch us. Soon after His resurrection He said to Mary Magdalene, "Touch me not; for I am not yet ascended to my Father . . ." (John 20:17 KJV).

Literally, the physical touch of Jesus can no more be felt. However, Jesus *did* say to His disciples, "These signs will accompany those who believe . . . *they* will lay hands on the sick and they will recover" (Mark 16:17-18, italics mine).

Jesus' touch, therefore, can still reach people, but now it is through the hands of His followers. The longing of those engaged in the healing ministry is:

"To be *His* hand extended
Reaching out to the oppressed.
Let me touch Him, Let me touch Jesus
That others may hear and be blessed."

This prayer-song reminds us that a two-way relationship is necessary for the Christian minister. With one hand he must, as it were, always be touching Jesus. Only then is he in a position to reach out and touch others. When this condition is fulfilled, however, he becomes a link between Jesus and the needy person. Obviously, no more than Mary Magdalene, can he literally touch the risen Lord. What is meant is that he must have a continually deep spiritual communion with Jesus, a keeping "in touch" with Him, spiritually. This will mean that those upon whom he lays his hands will really sense the presence of Jesus, and make spiritual contact with the One from whom all healing flows.

The laying on of hands is, therefore, one of the most important means of communicating divine healing. It stems from the example of Jesus himself and, consequently, is basic to the ministry today.

As we lay hands on the sick we must always make

explicit reference to Jesus; we must use His name. Then the gaze of the sick person, together with his faith, is immediately turned away from the minister to Jesus himself. I usually say to the sick person:

"Close your eyes. Relax! Don't strain. Don't get all worked up! Don't even try to pray—leave that to me. Simply think of Jesus in the best way you can. Picture Him coming to you in His white robes. In a moment, you will feel the touch of my hands. Let them be for you as the hands of Jesus himself."

I am trying to help the person to a deep personal relationship with Christ, which is the all-important factor in bringing wholeness. Testimony to what Jesus has done through this ministry abounds from every area I have visited. Physical sickness has been healed. A vicar from the Midlands writes:

A parishioner, Beryl, was due to go into hospital for a second mastectomy (removal of the breast), and also a lump had developed under her armpit. When she attended the meeting, she was very fearful, and only half hopeful when you laid your hands upon her and prayed for her. Afterwards she was examined by the doctor prior to the operation. "It appears to be dissolving," he commented incredulously, "but whatever you do, come back in a month for further examination." A month later doctors were unable to find any trace of cancer in her body. They are completely mystified as to what has happened to bring about this change in her condition. But Beryl knows! She cannot stop praising the Lord for His mercy and is praying for greater boldness in testifying to others of the healing power of Christ.

Mr. Houghton, of Skegness, Lincolnshire, brought a busload of people to a meeting in Stamford. He had, however, a deep need himself. For twenty years he had suffered a serious spinal disability which hospitals, specialists, tablets, heat treatment, and every other conceivable medical treatment had failed to alleviate. He later said that an "invisible force" prompted him to go forward for healing and that when I laid hands upon him he felt a "great heat" in his spine. He awoke the next morning to discover that all his pain had gone. He *ran* up the office steps instead of crawling up them. He now plays football, cricket, and golf with his teen-age boys and has even entered a tennis tournament. At forty-three years of age he feels fitter than a lot of men half his age. This healing took place three years ago and he is still going strong.

It has been a joy at meetings to see people able to completely discard wheelchairs, walking sticks, and other medical aids after the laying on of hands. One lady had been in St. Alban's hospital for six months with a fractured hip. Despite all this treatment she still came into the meeting hobbling on a stick. As I put my hands on her she fell to the ground under the power of the Holy Spirit. She rose up, forgot her stick, and walked back to her seat without any aid whatsoever. She has now been walking like that—and running too—for over five years.

A lady in Wisbech, Cambridgeshire, had been housebound for over two years and was literally carried into the meeting. After receiving the laying on of hands she wrote:

> My sticks, I have loaned to a young man recovering from a broken leg! I sleep through the night and can jump out of bed. I have skipped with a rope, run the length of my path with my dog, played trains with my grandson and even ridden a bicycle. I want to tell the whole world what Jesus has done for me!

Another incapacitated lady told me that, after ministry, she bounced into her doctor's office wearing high-heeled shoes.

I get all sorts of strange but pleasant surprises at meetings. One lady insisted on walking up to the front of the church carrying what, from a distance, looked like a huge piece of medieval armor. It turned out to be a medical saddle-leather jacket weighing nine pounds. The lady had brought it to give thanks to God that she no longer needed to wear it to support what had been a crumbling spine. How the congregation praised the Lord!

Another demonstration at a meeting was when a man who had been unable to walk properly began to tap dance on the church floor. Later he wrapped the crepe bandage with which his leg had been supported around the walking stick which had borne his weight, and laid them on the altar in a joyous thanksgiving.

This laying down of walking sticks has become quite a feature of my meetings. Such people have been able to resume normal life after ministry. Brian had never walked more than a few steps, but after prayer, in the sight of everyone, he actually walked the length of the Guildhall steps and out to a car on his own.

Many people have been able to resume normal life after meetings. Mrs. M. of Southend, after years of suffering with crippling arthritis, has been able to walk, do her housework, and even dig the garden. A mother, aged sixty-six, who had a crumbling spine, and who could not walk without pain, is now fit and has been swimming every day on her holiday. A daughter for whom doctors could do no more has, since ministry, taken a fellowship in dancing and passed with honors. The aged have not been left out. A lady of eighty-five years has told me of the healing of her cracked and broken ribs at the moment I laid hands on her. Doctors had told her that, at such an age, she was beyond their help.

Letters arrive at my home every day, relating what Jesus has done through the ministry of "healing hands." I like testimonies to be expressed that way because then I know that the healings have not been spurious—simply emotional suggestibility. They have stood the test of time and, in most cases, have been verified by doctors. For instance, a lady in Grays Thurrock, Essex, wrote, "I am happy to say that the hospital doctor says I have no diabetes and also my friend had hands laid on her for her angina and the doctor says that her heart is getting stronger."

We had letters also testifying in this way to the healing of stomach ulcers, angina, glandular complaints, and deafness. One lady, whose whole body was encased in a plaster cast, has amazed the hospital with such progress that it has been permanently removed.

Healing Hands

Children too have been much blessed, even when they have been too young or ill to know that they were being prayed for. A baby born blind received the healing touch of Jesus when I laid my hands upon her eyes. Within days, Moorfields Eye Hospital confirmed that irises had grown in her eyes, the glaucoma had subsided, and now, four years later, the little girl is able to see so well that she can ride a tricycle. Another child, Elizabeth, had cerebral palsy, and seemingly no future. Her parents write:

It is with great joy and thankfulness that we write to tell you of Elizabeth's progress. She is now talking so much, that we sometimes have to tell her to be quiet. Three years ago we were told that she would never speak, or in fact do anything at all. She is now at school (full-time) and is learning to read and write and do all the normal things that children do. It is wonderful to hear her singing carols and taking part in a nativity play. How good the Lord has been to us.

These and healings like them have been the result of faith in Jesus exercised by the parents, myself and the church.

This ministry, however, need not always be in the environment of a church service. As in the New Testament, it can be anywhere. One day, after a pastors' meeting, as I was walking out of a vicarage, a vicar mentioned to me that his wife was suffering from an infected throat. I was just about to put on my coat and actually had one arm in its sleeve. I reached out the other hand and touched her throat. It was instantly healed and as soon as she got into her car she was able to sing.

Not only the physically afflicted, but also the "broken-hearted" and the "bruised" have been touched by Jesus through this ministry. I have received news that when I was in Wrexham, Wales, a lady came suffering from a nervous breakdown and dearly wanting a baby. She was healed and is now expecting her first child. In Birmingham a lady had such bad nerves that she had been sick four or five times every day for nearly two years. She described herself as in a "living hell." She has testified: "Jesus cured my sickness the night you laid hands on me. I'll never be the same again. Thank you, Lord. My sickness has ended."

Many others have likewise been healed of nervous depression and fear.

It is not usual for me actually to *lay hands* on Satan's captives, the demon-possessed. In one meeting at Tunbridge Wells, Kent, however, I felt especially led by the Spirit to do so. The victim described her experience in a letter:

I had begun work for a new company. Before long I discovered that in the office were a number of girls attached to a spiritist circle. I joined them, read the literature and became fanatical about the whole thing. I dressed constantly in black with masses of rings and neck chains. My bouts of depression got worse and I became suicidal. It was on such a black day that I saw an advertisement for your meeting of Power, Praise and Healing. I felt drawn to attend. This service changed my life. When my turn for healing came I prayed, "If you are really there, God, help me now." As my eyes opened, my body seemed filled with something wonderful and, as I lay on the floor of the church, I could see the altar cross shining. I rose up feeling I was walking on air. From that day my depression disappeared. I renounced spiritism, became a Christian, and every aspect of my life has changed.

These are only a few of the hundreds of firsthand testimonies from my own ministry, that Jesus is healing the sick today through the laying on of hands. Once again we would emphasize that this is not simply a matter of a magical healing touch. Healing flows through a deep encounter and involvement with Jesus, as a person. It comes through a relationship with Him based on deep trust in His promises. We would—much like Peter in Acts 3:11, 16—say to people: "Do not look at us as if through our own power or holiness we had made this man walk. It is His name, through faith in His name, that these people have been given this perfect soundness in the presence of you all."

13

The All-Powerful Word

In the Bible tremendous emphasis is placed upon the power of God's voice. He only has to speak for things to happen. In the beginning, "God *said* 'Let there be light'; and there was light" (Gen. 1:3, italics mine).

God has promised that the power of His word will accomplish His purposes.

> So shall my word be that goes forth from my mouth;
> it shall not return to me empty, but it shall
> accomplish that which I purpose, and prosper in the
> thing for which I send it. (Isa. 55:11)

In the New Testament, we are told that in Jesus, "The Word became flesh and dwelt among us" (John 1:14).

There was, therefore, no limit to what Jesus could accomplish, simply by speaking. As we have seen, He spoke forgiveness to the penitent, deliverance to the captives, health to the sick, and life to the dead.

Even our *human* words, once they have been uttered, have power either to hurt or to help people. Sometimes they are still doing damage to the hearers or, more positively, encouraging them, years after they were actually spoken. How much more then do our words have power when He actually speaks through us! He has promised to give our words *His* power by placing *His* Word upon human lips.

> The word is nigh thee, even in thy mouth, and in thy heart: that is, the word of faith, which we preach. (Rom. 10:8 KJV)

Paul once said that he was pleased his hearers did not receive his message simply as the words of men, but as it truly was the word of God. (See 1 Corinthians 2.)

Words, therefore, like the laying on of hands, are of fundamental importance in the healing ministry. It is noticeable that following the example of Jesus, the apostles not only laid hands upon people, they also spoke God's healing word to them. We must do the same today. I have found inspired words to be an essential part of divine healing ministry.

It was the "word" which was so effective in the case of Nanette Pierce. This lady was wheeled into a meeting suffering from terminal cancer. She was a dark, pretty young woman, married, with two children. Her tragic condition was well known in her home town of Peterborough because the local newspaper had issued a special appeal to readers to bring her home from the U.S.A. so that she could die and be buried here. However, some months later the same newspaper carried a front-page headline: "Miracle." Reporters described how this lady was no longer expected to die. Apparently, after she attended one of my meetings, doctors discovered that all traces of the disease had disappeared.

She told newspaper reporters that the change had actually taken place when I had gone over to her and commanded, "Rise and walk, in the name of Jesus!"

"I couldn't help but obey him," she confessed. "I just got up!" So, a lady who looked such a pathetic wreck, rendered paralyzed by cancer, stood and then walked, for the glory of God. She had heard the word of God, unhesitatingly responded, and been healed. As an added bonus, her hair, which she had completely lost, immediately began to grow again. Her progress has continued.

In the power of Jesus, and with His word upon my lips, I have often addressed organs of the body and commanded them to respond to the healing power of Jesus. Healing has often resulted.

"Prostate gland, be healed!" I once cried. The patient, who had been passing blood, later wrote:

I went into the hospital for an exploration of my bladder. This was two months ago. Today I had to go to the hospital and was told I had a clean bill of health. Praise the Lord.

Sometimes, in the same spirit, I have rebuked sicknesses and commanded them to depart. Frequently the result has been remarkable. Arthritis, in particular, has yielded to this treatment. One lady wrote gratefully:

I was taken ill with severe arthritis of the spine in June of last year and, in spite of various hospital treatments, my position got worse, culminating in the Royal Free Hospital in London sending me here unable to help me in any way. I came to your mission at Wisbech. I am now greatly relieved. My family thinks a miracle has happened and I am greatly blessed.

Even cancers have shriveled up under the power of this ministry. Frequently, I have treated depression and fears in the same way. One testimony:

My mother, who was suffering from depression, was taking many drugs, tranquilizers, sleeping pills, etc. She stopped them due to your words and has been completely healed.

On that occasion my words had been: "You need to step out into the glorious liberty God has given you through His love." She did—and was delivered.

The word which speaks forgiveness still has great power for the remaking of the whole person. This has been a ministry particularly to those responding to the altar call which always follows the gospel message at my meetings. After each person has expressed penitence for their sins and publicly taken Christ as Savior, I have been able joyously to say: "On the authority of the Word of God, I am able confidently to declare to each one of you that your sins have been forgiven. You stand there in garments as white as snow for 'If we confess our sins, he is faithful and just to forgive us our sins and to cleanse us from all unrighteousness' " (1 John 1:9 KJV).

This was so in the case of young Jacky, who was the first person to come forward in response to the appeal at a rally in Southend, Essex. She was known throughout the school for her terrible temper, which eventually resulted in the headmaster actually expelling her. After my words to her the change in her was truly wonderful. Even unbelievers said, "My, you *have* changed, Jacky!" She was so thrilled that people were noticing the difference. Eventually the school took this transformed young person back again.

One lady came to the same meeting, at the invitation of her two sisters, themselves fairly recent converts. She told me that when she saw them raising their arms in worship she was truly embarrassed. Later in the meeting, however, she gave her heart to the Lord. "Now my sisters and I talk of the Lord freely and are forever praising Him for the healings which are taking place in our large family," she told me.

Family relationships have frequently been healed as this ministry of forgiveness has put all the past behind and given people the possibility of a new start together. When all parties have themselves received new wholeness of personality, they have been in a far better position to relate to the others. A healing like this happened when I visited Margate in Kent. A lady wrote:

I was blessed beyond words and felt the Holy Spirit fall on me. I want to thank you for bringing me to a greater commitment to Jesus. I went up for the healing of my broken marriage and am thanking God for healing.

After such a decision for Christ a man testified:

Jesus brought my wife and I back together and my family is now united in Jesus' name. In turn I have promised to bring my children up in a Christian home. I ask that my transformed life will be such a witness that my wife too will find Him as her Savior.

Another lady entered into a new relationship with her only daughter. She confessed to Jesus that she had been far too possessive of her and didn't want to let her go at the time of her marriage. After receiving God's forgiveness she felt free, released, and happy. She found that all the tension had gone from the relationship, which was now filled only with Jesus' love.

In my experience of ministering, the word of forgiveness has often been able even to lift depression. The peace of God has flooded the oppressed mind, binding up the broken heart and soothing all the bruises. Even physical sicknesses have been affected by forgiveness. One delighted convert wrote:

My body was becoming distorted with drugs, overeating and lack of exercise. I wasn't a nice person either. Then you told me about Jesus and I accepted Him as my Savior. Things started to change! I started to change from the inside. The injections have been stopped—the anti-depressants and sedatives went down the drain.

Perhaps Miss M.N. of Stamford sums up the difference Jesus makes in this respect:

I have never felt so clean and so different. I feel I can cope with life far easier now than I could before. I do not worry as much as I used to. I thank God for coming inside me and forgiving all my sins.

These selections from many testimonies show that the word of God still has power today both to heal and to forgive. Further, it is in fact *the only way* that today's captives can be set free from Satan's grip.

There is evidence that, at last, the medical profession is beginning to take seriously the reality of demon possession. Dr. Richard MacKarness, a British psychiatrist, wrote about "Medicine and the Devil" in the journal *Physician* and answered questions about his conclusions on a "Medikasset," which is widely circulated among our doctors. He said that certain cases he had met in his practice had led him to the conclusion that some people needed exorcism. These were: (a) when the onset of the psychiatric symptoms coincided with involvement in the occult, together with (b) the usual psychiatric treatment having failed and (c) when exorcism brought such relief that medication could be withdrawn.

He admitted that he had known cases where exorcism ministry had not benefited the patient, but felt that even so, it had done no harm.

"No one knows the ultimate cause of much mental illness" he had stated, therefore "the field is wide open."

In my own ministry, like that of my Lord, I have not sought for demon-possessed people, but have run into them as I have traveled.

In Ongar, Essex, I had hardly begun to minister to the sick when a young woman fell screaming at my feet. She began to knock her head on the floor and writhe about in terrible torment.

"Come out of her, and leave her alone, you unclean spirit," I commanded, "in the name of Jesus."

In a few moments she was free. The spiritual and emotional troubles which assailed her were over.

"It was like streams of clear, fresh water running through my being," she told an inquisitive newspaper reporter.

She was a Roman Catholic by denomination and, after reporting the incident to my bishop, I commended her to her priest for care. She has rejoiced in the Lord ever since.

In another town, by arrangement with the vicar, and by permission of the bishop, we actually held a special deliverance service for a young woman. She had been so involved in occultism and the drug scene that she had a black cross tattooed upside down upon her back. A sympathetic doctor had gone to great trouble to have it removed when she became a Christian. Still, however, she reacted violently to the name of Jesus and especially to the elements of bread and wine at Holy Communion. After the ministry of the delivering word she was able to praise the Lord and partake of the sacrament for the first time.

Later, a mission meeting in a large church in the Midlands was interrupted by the terrible noise of furniture being smashed at the rear of the church. A young man was, in fact, picking up chairs and crashing them one against the other. The minister and stewards tried to restrain him by pinning him to the floor. He shook them off with supernatural strength and ran from the building. Immediately I urged the congregation to pray.

"Destructive spirit, I bind you," I declared across the distance. "You shall not hurt him any more. In the name of Jesus, I loose him from your control."

We then prayed that the Spirit of God would direct his feet back to the church.

Surely enough, he returned. I discovered that he had been involved deeply in the meditational exercises of yoga. This had obviously been the point of the spirit's entry.

"I felt my body was going one way, despite all my mind wanted to do. I was taken over by something which used my body," he nervously explained.

It was all over in two minutes. He renounced the practice from the heart and, at the word of command, yet another spirit was dispatched to the pit to await the judgment of Christ.

In these days of the comeback of the supernatural, occultism is rampant. Innocent people, who do not appreciate the dangers, are getting involved in increasing numbers. Exorcism ministry is, therefore, increasingly vital. It is an essential part of divine healing ministry today. The power to deliver lies in the spoken word.

Through this ministry also, alcoholics have been set free, suicidals saved from death, drug addicts delivered, homes and families saved, depressives received new joy, spiritualists converted, and even smokers have been able to discard their last packet of cigarettes. Letters have just about burst their envelopes with joy. One woman wrote:

> After you had ministered to me, I could have skipped and danced back to my seat (after all for forty years these dreadful demons have had me in their power). I felt so light and free that I could hardly control my feet from dancing. Then came the acid test: coming home to the house where so much hate has been. I lifted my heart to God and went indoors believing He had done it. And He had, Brother Trevor, healed.

Perhaps one of the most unusual cases I ever had, which proved the power of the inspired spoken word, concerned a young married man classified as schizophrenic. He had lapsed into this state after losing his job and feeling unable to support his pretty wife and two young children. He had entered so deeply into a world of his own, that he could not be reached by normal conversation. It was the wife who first sought my help, and I persuaded her to bring him along to my meeting in Hadleigh, Essex, whatever his condition.

The situation did not look very promising because, at the beginning of the service, he was just wandering about the church mumbling incoherently to himself. I went up to him, but could obtain no rational replies to my questions.

Suddenly, however, I felt that I had to begin to prophesy. Promise after promise from God poured from my lips; all of them were especially for that young husband. I found I was declaring God's love for him and the certainty of His forgiveness. Eventually, I began to pray over him in other tongues which I did not even myself understand. Suddenly he looked up. Rationality had returned.

"I'm okay," he said. "Where am I? Where have I been?"

So his children had their father restored to them for Christmas and the family have since emigrated to the U.S.A. The word of God had reached a broken and bruised man where no human words could possibly have touched him.

All these incidents support my contention that liturgical structures and forms of service must leave a great deal of room for spontaneity. This ministry, to be effective, must be far from mechanical. The supernatural gift of discernment has to be sought, to really penetrate the area of need and minister accordingly, with hands and words. The correct verbal ministry is of very great importance for healing.

The words, however, must not be regarded as magical mumbo jumbo, but as the very words of God upon human lips. Once again, this is an extension of the ministry of Jesus in the world today. Words express personality. Jesus himself is met through the words of the preacher and healer, when they are, in fact, in harmony with the Bible's own message. Ultimately, however, it is Jesus who must be trusted to accomplish that which He has promised. It is *He* who must be obeyed as He speaks through His inspired servants. Now, however, He has no voice but that which comes through "anointed" human mouths. Therefore we pray, "Take my lips and let them be filled with messages from *Thee*."

God is still speaking supernatural healing and deliverance in the world today. "To day if ye will hear his voice, harden not your heart . . ." (Ps. 95:7-8 KJV).

14

Healing by Remote Control

The revival taking place within the church has led to a rediscovery of the gifts of the Holy Spirit, especially those listed by Paul in his first letter to the Corinthians: the word of knowledge, faith, gifts of healing, working of miracles, prophecy, discerning of spirits, various tongues, and the interpretation of tongues. Paul insisted that the functioning of these gifts is as closely related as the way in which the various organs of the human body work together. They are interdependent upon each other.

We have been focusing our attention especially on the gift of healing within the body of Christ. We have seen that this often includes exorcism or deliverance ministry. We have also seen how supernatural *faith* functions in relation to healing and that the gift of miracles also has its place. This is because healing is usually a gradual process; when it is instantaneous, however, it passes into the realm of "miracle." I have mentioned also how, in at least one instance, it was the gift of prophecy which was used to heal a man. In my experience, many people have been helped to receive healing by the use of this gift which has directed the word of God to the exact point of need. *Discernment*, particularly of the presence of evil spirits, is absolutely vital in healing. I have also indicated that I have often used the gift of *tongues* when praying for sick people. When the body of the church is ministering to its sick members, such helpful use of gifts may come from any Christian in the assembly. Indeed the gift of healing itself may be given to any spiritually sensitive member of the body. The use of all the gifts, however, must be in submission to the eldership of the church, to whom God has given responsibility for discipline, order, and government.

The gift of the word of knowledge certainly cannot be omitted from any study of divine healing. It is being widely used today to bring healing to every area of need. Once, when I was using this gift, a newspaper reporter, obviously at a loss for words, described it as "healing by remote control." Kathryn Kuhlman, in particular, was used in healing ministry in this way.

In the setting of a meeting it is usually, but not necessarily exclusively, the minister who is anointed for these utterances. Often it is while he is in worship, prayer, or even in the process of preaching, that he begins to "sense" that the Lord is healing people. His duty then is to declare *what God is actually doing*. Kathryn Kuhlman was so sensitive to the Spirit that she could even point to the exact area of a vast auditorium where the healing was taking place. This ministry is one of *revelation* and is not accompanied by the laying on of hands. People respond, not to receive ministry, but to verify and give thanks for what the Lord has already done.

The minister has to be particularly sensitive to the Spirit because the door is wide open to the possibility of simply using hit-or-miss methods. The skeptic can also point out that by the sheer law of averages, especially in a very large gathering, there are almost bound to be people with fairly common afflictions. The possibility of suggestible people excitedly running forward *thinking* that they are the ones being healed is also very obvious. For this reason the more specific and detailed the minister can be, the better. Kathryn Kuhlman also used to have doctors present to verify healings, before miracles were announced. Abuse has to be avoided for the sake of the honor of the Lord.

When asked just how she knew what God was doing, Kathryn Kuhlman used to say that she could not describe the process—she just knew. Once again, the curious must be told that there are no techniques which can be learned, no shortcut to this power. It is a gift for those upon whom God wishes to bestow it. Sensitivity to God, however, is a real priority.

I have found that I just cannot turn this ministry on when I want to! For me, sometimes it is there and sometimes it is not. I need to feel very inspired and unhurried to be used in this way. Laying on of hands is the normal way of divine healing; the word of knowledge is a special gift, resulting in special miracles.

When I am privileged to be used in this ministry, I stand, with my eyes closed, deeply concentrated and wonderfully aware of God. I must not be distracted. Then I become sensitive to various areas of my own body, as if there were a pain or disease there. I then say that God is healing someone of a need in that area. As I begin to speak often I am given more details, about the history of the complaint, or other factors which will help in identifying the particular person whom God is touching. Sometimes I am given pictures, for instance, of a baby dying at home, or of a twisted foot, or chains holding someone to a dominant person. I have no control over how long this will continue before I am brought back to earth. I usually then ask people who know that they have been healed to stand and thank the Lord.

There are, however, occasions when healed people just cannot restrain themselves from immediately praising the Lord.

"My foot, my foot, I can move it! I really can," shouted an excited girl in a marquee at Cheadle where I was ministering.

She had cause for joy as her club foot had not moved since she was born and she was actually awaiting an operation which had only a slight chance of success.

"I can hear," deaf people have exclaimed—and so the miracles have multiplied.

On one occasion, at Wolverhampton, I received ten such words of knowledge and all were verified before I left the area the next day.

Once again, however, I like time to elapse, to make sure, for Jesus' sake, that the miracles are genuine. Only then do I declare them in public testimony. This usually means that people write to me after a mission is over. Sample letters read:

Healing by Remote Control

I would like to pass on some news of a miracle of healing that came to me at Wisbech, when, by word of knowledge, you described my symptoms. After keeping away from doctors for three years, I suddenly needed six within the space of three months, and was taken ill twice when away from home and had to send for help. Constant bilious attacks, a colitis condition, and agonizing pain in the small of the back—sometimes causing me to lie on the floor to try to find a position to be out of pain. The night before Wisbech I spent hours with a "water works" condition, exactly as you described it. From the moment you mentioned these symptoms they vanished completely. I still did not believe it and had already arranged for a checkup in the R.A.F. hospital. After a week of intensive investigations they pronounced me completely free and healthy.

All praise once more to our fantastic heavenly physician.

We praise the Lord for the wonderful disappearance of a lump on a lady's breast which was feared to be malignant. By word of knowledge you said it would go—and it has!

Mrs. S.N. of Basildon had healing of memories through a word of knowledge on Canvey Island. She had been distressed for years by the memory of the loss of her son. Now she has peace. Praise the Lord.

A letter from Stoke-on-Trent described how I had revealed the healing of four major illnesses:

You also discovered a bad chain forged between a mother and child—which you promised would be broken and you said "there will be nothing but love from now on." That chain has been growing thicker and heavier for years between my daughter and me. She came home for Christmas and the love has been wonderful.

From Spalding came a letter:
You said, "There is a person here suffering from sinus trouble for fifteen years." That was me. You declared me healed so I threw away my nose drops. The sickness just went. Praise the Lord.

Letters followed my visit to St. John's Church, Bradford, telling—among other things—of the healing of "someone on my right having trouble with his rectum" and another with a "relationship with a difficult mother." A letter from Lincolnshire spoke of the healing of a long-standing kidney complaint.

These are just drops in the ocean of what is happening. Whatever skeptics may say, there is no doubt, from all the evidence we have, that thousands of people all over the world are being healed today through this supernatural ministry of revelation.

The most serious objection to this ministry, from a Christian point of view, is that it savors of magic. It seems, on the surface, that the healing "just happens" whether the person likes it or not—that there is no necessity for personal faith in the Lord Jesus Christ. This, however, is far from true. The minister in no way claims to be healing people himself, either by his words or his actions. His task is to reveal what *the Lord is doing*. This presumes that he has himself a very deep relationship with the Lord and supernatural faith in what He is able to accomplish. The ministry of revelation is also one of obedience, as the minister launches out in his utterances, prepared, if necessary, to appear to be "a fool for Christ's sake." He *has* to act, whatever the response. The whole ethos is one of praise and adoration to the risen Christ who is believed to be powerfully present and moving in the midst. All is done in His name.

The response to the ministry also involves real faith. The exact description of the illness, when it exactly fits the needs and location of a particular person, is not magic but a tremendous boost to the sick one's *faith*. The affected person must, however, have prior belief that Jesus is alive and has power to heal today. The response he makes is indicative of a relationship with Him. The afflicted person also must claim and grasp the healing, otherwise he will lose it! It all happens so quickly and wonderfully that it can appear to be "magic." Closer examination, however, reveals that all the principles which distinguish divine healing from mere supernaturalism are implicit in the ministry. A relationship with Jesus—faith—love and obedience all work together to bring about remarkable, breath-taking results.

Another field where the word of knowledge is very important is that of healing by personal counseling. We noticed when studying the ministry of Jesus that He often had private sessions with people, which were essential for their salvation.

When I was engaged in divine healing ministry as vicar of St. Paul's, Hainault, I used to set aside at least six hours every week for personal consultations. This is a duty which no pastor can avoid. In those days I had a ministry based in one particular place, with *pastoral* responsibility for those committed to my care. I was far more often at home than I was away, and so people knew where to find me. Now, in my itinerant ministry, counseling sessions are much more difficult to arrange. When I am at home, I must rest and give my time to my wife and family. When I go to other churches, I am ministering to those who are under the care of other shepherds, to whom it is my duty to relate. Nevertheless, I have found the counseling ministry still to be of great importance, especially for those who are not being healed by other ministry, or who have deep, personal problems.

It is often impossible, in a large meeting, to get that real discernment which is necessary for the healing of deep-seated afflictions. The bruised and broken-hearted also usually need time spent with them alone. Their healing can be likened to the peeling of an onion, when layer after layer has to be taken off before the heart of the matter is revealed. Like the peeling of an onion, such ministry is seldom accomplished without the shedding of tears! Those delivered from evil spirits also need a lot of counseling in the art of spiritual warfare before they can be regarded as healed.

Desperate people often seek counseling immediately after a meeting, but I am usually too tired to engage in a ministry which requires deep concentration. I have found it best, if possible, to make a special time, when, unhurriedly, we can together seek the Lord. In itinerent ministry I have always felt it important that the regular pastor should also be there, for he often sheds light on the problem and also has responsibility for following up the case. Indeed, rarely will I ever see a person without the consent of the man who has the responsibility for the regular pastoral care of that person.

Much prayer must precede such interviews, for we are going to seek the mind of the Lord. When general conversation has helped the seeker to feel relaxed, I pray with all who are present. I ask the Lord for the supernatural gifts of the Spirit which we shall need to bring deep healing. We recollect the presence of the Lord and especially ask for the word of knowledge which will reveal the real area of need and any blockages to healing. It is essential for me to have one ear open to the needy person and the other open to the Lord.

Often, immediately following this prayer, I find I want to ask questions. On the surface they may seem very mundane, but time after time I have discovered them to be real words of knowledge, going straight to the heart of the problem. For instance, if I have felt led to ask the person where he is in Christian fellowship, I have usually discovered that the real problem is that either the person is a spiritual vagrant, belongs to a church where he is being spiritually stoned to death, is engaged in broken relationships in the church, or is "at war" with his pastor.

I may, on the other hand, have been impelled to ask how the person's marriage is progressing. Then often tests have shown that I have immediately "hit the nail on the head." The question, "What is the relationship between you two?" has sometimes revealed adultery, immorality, lesbianism, or homosexuality. Questions such as these: "When did you last lose a loved one?"; "What job do you do?"; "What is your financial position?"; "What drugs are you taking?"; "When did you last engage in the occult?" have, time after time, pinpointed the need. Secular psychoanalysis invites hours of talking as the psychiatrist probes associated thoughts and fears in order to find the deep cause of emotional distress. In Christian counseling, however, we can begin with the faith that God knows everything about the situation. As the Psalmist said:

> O Lord, thou hast searched me, and known me. Thou knowest my downsitting and mine uprising, thou understandest my thoughts afar off. Thou compassest my path and my lying down and art acquainted with all my ways. For there is not a word in my tongue, but lo, O Lord, thou knowest it altogether. Thou has beset me behind and before and laid thine hand upon me. . . . Thou hast covered me in my mother's womb. . . . My substance was not hid from thee, when I was made in secret, and curiously wrought in the lowest parts of the earth. . . . Search me, O God, and know my heart: try me, and know my thoughts: And see if there be any wicked way in me, and lead me in the way everlasting (Ps. 139:1-5, 13, 15, 23-24 KJV).

God knows everything about us, and by the Holy Spirit

He is willing and able to impart this knowledge to us for the healing of the whole person.

Obviously, however, no matter how the interview begins, the sufferer must be given plenty of time to talk. This is therapeutic in itself. There is a real "unwinding," often accompanied by release of emotion. I have learned to appear impassive as people have cried but nevertheless I always have a large box of tissues ready in my counseling room.

The conversation, however, must not be allowed simply to wander aimlessly on. The counselor has to sense where the Lord is leading and direct the train of thought along the right lines. Sometimes it can be like playing the children's game of "hunt the thimble." In this game onlookers who know the location of the hidden object cry "hot" or "cold" or "getting warmer" as the seeker moves closer to or farther away from the article for which he is looking. Similarly, as a counseling interview proceeds I begin to sense whether I am getting nearer to or farther away from the root of the sufferer's problem. Once I feel I am really getting "warm," I pursue my line relentlessly, no matter how much it hurts the counselee, lovingly but firmly ignoring their subconscious attempts to change the conversation to a less painful subject.

This is once again "healing by remote control," but here the control is not over geographical distance but over thought, words, attitudes, and emotions.

Sometimes more than one interview is necessary because either the patient and listener have reached saturation point, or the Lord has accomplished all He knows is wise for the present time. The healing process, however, has definitely begun.

Each interview should conclude with definite action related to the factors the Lord has revealed by word of knowledge. This may be a period of definite confession of penitence for sin, followed by words of absolution. Perhaps the laying on of hands and/or anointing with oil will be ministered with prayers related to the specific needs uncovered. Painful memories of traumatic experiences may have to be brought for the healing power of the Lord to soothe away. There may have to be definite forgiveness of people who have caused hurt—parents, husbands, wives, pastors, and even political leaders. Resentments and bitterness towards, for example, the woman with whom a husband committed adultery, a father who committed incest, a thief who stole one's dearest possessions or a congregation who dismissed a pastor, must be dealt with very ruthlessly. On the other hand, the seeker may have to leave the interview room firmly resolved to ask forgiveness of those whom he has wronged.

In the case of marital stress, the other partner may have to be seen. Sometimes the "patient's" doctor, pastor, psychiatrist, or social worker may have to be contacted—of course always with the patient's consent. Debts may have to be settled or work obtained. Relationships may have to be put right. The possibilities are limitless.

Sometimes the result is not that which the needy person expected. I have been called to counsel several people who were thought to be demon possessed. They have come fully expecting the interview to conclude with deliverance ministry. However, after I have discovered that the real need has been elsewhere, I have acted accordingly. Sometimes I have been shown the Lord intends to teach the person many new spiritual lessons through struggle rather than simply instantaneously ending their problems.

This ministry is so demanding of time that I have found it necessary to train others to help me in counseling. In fact, a counseling course is always held in every church where I intend to mission. (See 2 Corinthians 12:7-10.) I feel that every mature Christian should be able to engage in this wonderful ministry.

Once a church has an army of counselors, I am able to call upon them to help people whom I discern to need this ministry, even while my meeting is in progress. At St. Paul's, Hainault, the counseling room was always in use during my meetings and this ministry often continued long after I had returned to the vicarage to go to bed.

My wife has become a very gifted counselor and has a most inspired personal ministry. At the World Conference on the Holy Spirit in Switzerland, she helped several people in this way. One young couple were completely mystified about the terrible way life was collapsing all around them. They had even been driven to contemplating suicide. My wife was given supernatural knowledge that they had been cursed. This revelation really rang the bell with them. The practical action which ensued was powerful prayer wherein the Lord broke the occult forces which had been holding them. Story after story could be recounted of such supernatural insights in our counseling ministry, which has always resulted in healing, when all other ministry has failed.

The world today is full of desperately needy people, who long to be made whole. God, in His mercy, has committed to His people the ministry of divine healing. Praise Him! He has also given us the supernatural gifts of the Spirit freely at our disposal, to enable us to function with real power. The word of knowledge is one of the most wonderful of these abilities.

15

Miracles Across Miles

It is certainly right that we should seek healing for ourselves. The teaching of the whole Bible is that sickness of the body, mind, and soul is an evil invasion of our lives, which we are far better without. It is natural and inevitable, therefore, that we should seek to be rid of it by every God-given means. We look to God to heal us, not only for our own sake, but for the sake of others. Fit and well, we are not a burden to other people, can serve God more effectively, and bring glory to His holy name. There is nothing sinful or selfish about desiring to be well and acting to keep that way!

I have, however, been very moved at meetings by the deep, often agonizing concern which people have shown for sick relatives, friends and even strangers whom God has laid on their hearts. Such compassion is surely born of God's love, filling our human lives. This is all the more wonderful to see, in days when individuals seem to matter less and less, to be numbers rather than names, and when human life has often seemed to be regarded as cheap. It is refreshing to know that the attitude of a man to whom I was talking in a Cornish café who said, "I would shoot the lot" is not the only way of regarding chronically sick people in contemporary society.

Human compassion for sick people stands out clearly in the pages of the New Testament. As we have seen, Jesus always welcomed it and acted to heal sick loved ones, even though they were many miles away.

We noted previously that people did come to Jesus asking for healing for their sick friends. When this happened, as in the case of a nobleman who asked Jesus to heal his son, Jesus did not reply in words like: "Thank you for telling me. I am pleased you are showing such concern. You can now go away and next time I am in prayer to my Father I will ask Him to heal your son. If it is His will I am sure He will do so, otherwise I'm sorry but you will have to accept the situation as it is."

No! The nobleman was very specific in his request and Jesus very definite in reply. The important words uttered by the Savior were: "As *your* faith, so be it unto *him*," and his son recovered that very hour.

This was ministry by proxy. It coheres with all we have seen to be fundamental in divine healing ministry. There was nothing magical about this healing; it involved a relationship with Jesus, obedience, love and faith in His willingness and ability to heal. However, because the sick person couldn't actually be there, and because Jesus could not himself go, the relationship of faith had to be "on behalf of" the sick person. The nobleman was literally a "stand-in," a representative or substitute for his son.

It is interesting also to see that Jesus did not find it necessary to lay hands on people who came on behalf of others. His word of command was sufficient to bring healing. As the centurion said on another such occasion: "Speak the word only and my servant shall be healed." I have followed this Bible pattern all over the world. I have usually given the opportunity for this ministry by proxy near the end of my meeting, after seeing the power of God move upon sick people actually present. This has helped to build up that extra faith necessary in believing God will work miracles across the miles.

In answer to all letters I receive asking for healing prayer, I reply pointing out that, if possible, the sick person should receive direct ministry. I have promised, however, that if this is not possible, I will minister by proxy. I have found it helpful to give a time, usually ten P.M. and, if possible, a date, when not only I, but a whole congregation of Spirit-filled believers will trust our Lord for the healing. I have asked the petitioner, and, if possible, the sick person, to "tune in to God" with us at that time and expect a miracle. So I go to every meeting with a list of the people who will be joining us in prayer across the miles that evening.

On arrival at each meeting I usually also find a pile of letters requesting prayer for absent friends. I presume also that nearly everybody in the congregation will have a burden for someone known to them who is sick.

At approximately ten P.M., knowing that people in other parts of the world are joining us, though at different times by their clocks, I gather all those needs together.

I briefly explain the principles of ministry by proxy, and ask people to *stand and believe* for those whose names they have placed on the papers awaiting my arrival. I ask others to stand and believe with me for the people whose names I have brought and which I will read out. Finally I invite anyone who is really believing in God to stand for any friend or relative whom He has laid on their hearts. By this time very few people are still seated!

This "exercise" only takes a few moments, and the next vital factor is to get our spiritual sights into focus on the power of our risen, glorified Lord. So we praise and adore Him. As these praises are ringing heavenwards, I begin to ask God for the gift of that supernatural faith which will move mountains of sickness. Names are called out, and amidst all the praise I am shouting, "Sickness go, in the name of the Lord." "Demons flee, in Jesus' name." "Blind, see! Deaf, hear! Lame, rise up and walk!" "Depression, we break your power! Fears, flee." "Speak the word from the heavenlies, Lord, and these people shall be healed."

When I feel so led, I lead praise, adoration and thanksgiving to the Lord for all we believe He has done.

The evidence I have is that truly He *has* done great things through this ministry.

In Finland relatives had been urgently called to the hospital where their loved one was nearing the end with terminal cancer. They had come to be with her when she died. However, miles away in Helsinki, another relative had taken a different course. She was standing—and believing Jesus. The critically ill lady began to make an astonishing and rapid recovery. We met Finnish friends recently in the world conference at Switzerland who told us that this lady is now living a normal life with no trace of cancer in her body.

On another occasion in Ireland, I was given rather a

shock during this ministry. As I was praying powerfully, one intercessor suddenly fell with a tremendous crash onto the stone floor at the church. Angels must have hurried to put invisible spiritual cushions under her, for she was not hurt. Her friend, however, was *healed*. Florence later wrote:

> As I stood in the prayer line, thinking of her and what Jesus can do, the Lord touched me, and I fell down with a terrible bang in the Spirit. Well, since then, she has phoned to say that the bleeding has stopped and she hasn't taken a tablet since. She is really cured. We have praised the Lord in tears and laughter.

In this ministry the Lord has overcome all language difficulties. He *had* to do so when I was in Spain. A remarkable miracle resulted. It involved a very sick woman on the other side of the country who didn't even know that faith was being exercised on her behalf at a meeting I was holding in a believer's house. I learned the next day that this very sick woman just couldn't understand what was happening to her as she lay in bed. All she knew was that at about ten P.M. she began to feel very much better. She could hardly believe it, but, as strength flowed into her body and new life into her limbs, she decided to see if she could get out of bed. She easily succeeded, and was discovered, early in the morning, to be doing her housework—for the first time in ten years. Excited relatives asked me if I would go to visit her. The dear lady had been told that her healing was the result of my ministry and so desperately wanted to thank me. I went to her, and, as I walked in through the door, she flung her arms 'round me and wept for joy. We couldn't communicate at all, but I managed to convey to her that it was Jesus who had made her whole. She surrendered her new life to Him.

So the testimonies have flowed into our home, regularly bringing news of miracles across the miles:

- a lady's cataracts disappeared so she doesn't now need to wear glasses and is taking lessons in sculpture.
- a growth in the stomach disappeared.
- a lady of ninety years freed from hallucinations.
- internal surgery not needed.
- eye healed of a terrible disease.
- four-year-old child recovered from serious illness.
- back instantly healed of severe pain.
- lady with serious Parkinson's disease now doing all her own housework and also shopping for elderly people.
- the very next day patient was happy and relaxed and cancer in the face began to go.
- barren daughter now expecting a baby.
- lady fully recovered from brain hemorrhage.
- depression completely gone.
- husband's ulcer disappeared and no operation needed. Wife did not need threatened hysterectomy.
- lady severely incapacitated with multiple sclerosis walked three miles next day.
- slipped disc instantly healed.

- "nerve degeneration in feet miraculously" healed, says hospital.
- man's eyes healed; he could hardly believe it.

One letter reads:

The change since last Tuesday evening is wonderful. She wakens up and wants to get out of her chair. Or she will sit in the garden—so happy and contented. She's laughing and singing and getting into mischief—eating well and sleeping better. She even asked to go swimming again after months.

The last few years have brought a continual flow of blessing through this ministry as miracles have happened across the miles. Like all pastors, I had always prayed for the sick in the customary manner. I did so, however, with no authority and little expectancy. How I praise Him for all He has shown me, in the last few years, about how *really* to minister by proxy faith for sick people. This is since I have had the courage to launch out in obedience to the biblical pattern. I have entered into the realm of the supernatural—the miraculous.

His Name is Jesus, Jesus!
Sad hearts weep no more!
He heals the broken-hearted,
opens wide the prison door.
He is able to deliver evermore.

To minister and receive divine healing over a distance, through the power of the spoken word, requires great faith, I have found. Many people are helped by some material sense-aid. It is recorded in Acts 19:11-12 that Paul was willing that people should use handkerchiefs and aprons as a help to their faith. By their use the Lord wrought special miracles of healing and deliverance.

I have taken this up in my own ministry and, in my letters to people who request "absent" healing, I have freely offered "anointed prayer cloths" as a help in case of need. In fact I have received the most unusual objects through the mail—strands of hair, broaches, underwear, photographs, and even "lucky" charms. In medieval days, saints' relics were so used. We haven't yet had any of these! I have replied suggesting handkerchiefs as at least they are biblical.

Even so, my offering of anointed prayer cloths once brought a storm of protests from local ultra-Protestant ministers, especially as they wrongly thought I was actually *selling* "Trevor Dearing blessed hankies." Quite a discussion followed with my bishop who, in the end, didn't want either to approve or disapprove the method! The many letters of healing I have received, however, have encouraged me to continue the practice. The Lord has seemed pleased to bless the people whose faith has been helped in this way. Some typical letters:

> I feel I must write. I've been an arthritic for a number of years, with other troubles. Now I have received a tremendous improvement over the last few weeks, after receiving a prayer cloth. Now the fear of being alone that I have suffered this last twelve months has completely gone.

Just a line to thank you for your prayer cloth that you kindly sent. I am glad to say that the ulcer on my left leg has been healed!

I wrote to you about my mother Mrs. Xigi, who lives in Greece and was suffering with cancer. I sent her the prayer cloth you sent me and I am happy to tell you that by the grace of our Lord she is better. The lump has completely gone.

I have to testify to healing and help we have been receiving through prayer, belief and the use of the prayer handkerchief. My wife's blood pressure continues to be normal.

Evidence is that the Lord has been pleased also to heal through the use of other media. One is the use of television programs. I have received several messages about absent people being healed while watching my recorded debates about healing. One man and his wife were healed of a water infection, blood pressure, diabetes, thyroid trouble and fibroids in this way. Others have been healed while listening to my tape-recorded messages and services. One person found that actually touching the tape was the avenue for healing power from God.

Here we come nearer than anywhere else to the magical in divine healing ministry. However, I have done everything possible to prevent this. Every prayer cloth I give away has carefully prepared instructions for its use. I make it very clear that the cloth *itself* contains no magical power. They have, however, been prayed over and consecrated in healing meetings and, therefore, some people can see them as extensions of that service, in the same way as the "Reserved Sacrament" is an extension of the Holy Communion service.

Whatever one may think about such theology, the whole emphasis in my instructions is that it is Jesus alone who heals. I urge the sufferers to read the gospel story and put their faith in the risen Christ. I urge them also to confess their sins to Him and take Him as their Savior before using the cloth. I suggest that they place the cloth, if possible, on the affected part, and command the sickness to go in the name of Jesus. I instruct them to give thanks to Him for what He has done. That this message gets across is shown by the following letter:

I was thrilled to receive a prayer cloth as I've heard about them. I know there is no magic in it but it is an aid to faith. I used my prayer cloth doing all the things you told me. I put my cloth on my chest and rebuked the enemy. I kept the cloth next to my chest, inside my clothes. Jesus gave me strength and healing.

Thank God, He understands us. He knows whereof we are made. He remembers that we are but dust.

He is so merciful and gracious that He lovingly accommodates himself to our weakness, and as we offer our little faith to Him—it is Jesus who makes us whole—as by proxy ministry, or "faith-aids," He works miracles across the miles.

16

Divine Healing and the World of Medicine

From its beginning, my divine healing ministry has inevitably meant my being involved with the medical profession. Their response to my activities has varied from apathy and opposition to friendship and cooperation. The doctors whose practices were first affected were those whose offices were within easy traveling distance of my church at Hainault. When the opportunity arose some of them actually suggested to interested patients that they might well benefit from a visit to my services. They had the satisfaction of seeing many supernatural healings. A London doctor, interviewed by the *National Enquirer*, spoke about a lady who had a heart attack:

I prescribed digitalis to strengthen her heartbeat. Patients with this condition seldom recover completely.

On October 10 last year, Miss B. went to see Rev. Dearing and was cured. I can see no other way she could have been cured other than by divine healing.

Dr. Carlisle of Southend often informed me of the way in which God had blessed his patients to whom I had ministered, some of whom had been suffering from very acute and chronic conditions, including multiple sclerosis, muscular dystrophy, mental illness, and cancer.

When I left St. Paul's, Hainault, in order to travel throughout the world, I encountered more people whose divine healing began with suggestions by their doctors that they might benefit from such ministry. One, whom I had exorcised in a most dramatic demonstration of victorious spiritual warfare, gave public testimony during my mission in Ongar Parish Church, Essex. Her doctor was actually sitting in the congregation to hear her declare how the intervention of God had completely transformed her from being an "incurable psychotic" into a radiant wife and mother.

As my travels increased, so the number of medical practitioners with whom I could have fellowship multiplied. Dr. Curtis of Matlock, Derbyshire, was so impressed by what he saw in Power, Praise, and Healing services that he arranged for me to address a special meeting of his colleagues to discuss divine healing, exorcism, and medicine.

I have obviously welcomed all these contacts with the world of medicine. I realized that if divine healing is to make sense today, its relationship to medical science has to be fully considered. The latter offers to people vast resources of knowledge, technique, and medication which have proved to be of tremendous value in alleviating sickness, pain, and distress. Further, while divine healing is still in the process of making a comeback, medical men have already won a place of esteem and respect unparalleled by any other profession. Contact with the world of medicine is therefore essential for all those embarking on a work of healing in the world today.

It has been especially gratifying to see the way in which the medical profession has begun to take divine healing seriously. Articles discussing it have recently appeared in medical journals and doctors have joined in the church's debate about exorcism. Their interest has made progress towards better understanding and actual cooperation a practical possibility.

It is not always easy, however, to relate the Bible-based insights of the divine healing ministry to those of modern, rationalistic science. Some Christians would even consider it to be an impossible task, because the Bible is basically opposed to such worldly logic. Paul strongly emphasized this truth when writing to the Corinthians:

> Where is the wise? where is the scribe? where is the disputer of this world? hath not God made foolish the wisdom of this world? . . . God hath chosen the foolish things of the world to confound the wise. . . . (1 Cor. 1:20, 27 KJV)

This reiterates the teaching of Jesus: "I thank thee, Father, Lord of heaven and earth, that thou hast hidden these things from the wise and understanding and revealed them to babes; yea, Father, for such was thy gracious will" (Matt. 11:25-26 KJV).

In the light of this teaching how can Christians relate to

doctors on the subject of "supernatural" divine healing, when doctors have been rigorously schooled to base all their efforts upon the foundation of a scientific rationalism which excludes all possibility of healing "miracles"?

I have always known, of course, that no person can ever fully embrace Christian truth without the enlightment given by the Holy Spirit. However, I have never understood this to mean that Christianity is *irrational*, totally devoid of reason, or absurd. Jesus actually taught us to love God with all our *minds* (Luke 10:27), that is, with our reasoning faculties. God does not ask us to abandon reason, because He actually created human minds. If we cannot present our gospel message in a way in which unbelievers can understand it, then no one will ever be converted! It is for this reason that Christians, seeking to communicate their beliefs to people living in a scientific age, must ask God for the gift of "words of wisdom" (1 Cor. 12:8, James 1:5). I pray for a double portion of this gift when trying to communicate the truths of divine healing to doctors.

I have, in fact, always tried to explain to them that my ministry is based upon a Christian conception of God. I have actually pointed to the field of medical research to urge that it is reasonable to believe that there are dimensions of existence beyond the physical, material world of our sense experience. For instance, bacteria affected human beings in many ways before the invention of the microscope made it possible to see these infinitely minute microbes. In a similar way, Christians, with their spiritual eyes, have a definite experience of a spiritual dimension of life which is beyond our natural sense experience. At its highest, most noble and best, our spiritual experience is of *God himself*.

I have further explained that, as Christians, we do not believe in God as a vague abstraction; we think of Him in the way He manifested himself to us in His Son, Jesus Christ. Jesus, we know, spent much of His time healing the sick, loving and caring for those around Him. In view of this, Christians can confidently assume that the God and Father of our Lord Jesus Christ usually wills to heal sick people, for He said, "He who has seen me, has seen the Father" (John 14:9).

Once I have established that it is reasonable to believe in a God who heals, I usually turn to the second basic belief of divine healing—that we can be supernaturally healed because we are *spiritual* as well as *physical* beings.

Doctors, I feel, are in danger of seeing man mainly as a mass of valves, tubes, bones, and tissues, simply a complicated organism. Although they generally acknowledge also the inter-relationship between mind and body, especially in psychogenic disorders, they can still leave out the *spiritual* aspect of our lives. They must realize that many sane people claim not only to have consciousness of earthly things, but also to have an experience of a God who vitally affects their lives. Christians feel that a *complete* view of man is that he is a *spiritual*, psychosomatic being, in which body, mind, and soul interact either for health or for sickness.

From this point of view, spiritual health is of crucial importance for the well-being of the whole person.

Divine healing, then, is the entry of the health- and life-giving Spirit of God into our lives, through the gateway of our own God-given spirits. If this invasion is complete it can have incalculable, beneficial effects upon the whole of our beings. There are literally no limits to what can be accomplished. (See Ephesians 3:14-21.) Therefore, when I minister this healing I regard myself simply as a point of contact between the Spirit of God and the patient's own limited sensory perception. By the use of touch, words, and other encouragements to faith, I assist the sick person to receive God's healing power. The healing process is no magic. It involves a personal response to God based on a trust and love which issues in obedience. When this is present, the sick person opens up to God, and all the healing resources of heaven flood his being.

When I am explaining *exorcism* ministry to doctors, I can draw yet another parallel between medical healing and divine healing. I describe how a person's spirit can be just as vulnerable to an invasion by evil spirits as his body is open to penetration by germs. For this reason, people involving themselves in the occult are literally going into the middle of a terrible spiritual epidemic to which exorcism is the only answer. This ministry is a "specialist" branch of divine healing, involving the experience of a spiritual consultant. His spiritual surgery drives out the evil forces by the power of God's Word. This not only brings health to the soul but an end to related disturbances in both the mind and body. It always has to be followed by an infilling of the soul with the cleansing, life-giving "oxygen" of God's own Holy Spirit.

It follows from this description of divine healing that it is not basically opposed to the world of medical science and that it does not necessarily disparage or criticize its methods. What it does say, however, is that because man is a spiritual being, there are more ways of bringing healing to him than simply the physical. Those who believe in divine healing share a fundamental principle with the medical profession—that sickness is an evil invasion of human life. They further urge that Christianity and medicine should cooperate together, using every means of healing at their disposal to aid sick and unhappy people.

My experience on my travels is that not only many doctors but also *some Christians* need convincing about the value of cooperation between medicine and the church in the field of healing. This is not only because some believers fail to realize that our heavenly Father is God of the *natural* as well as the supernatural, but also because they see trust in medical healing methods as contradictory to faith in God's own ability to heal. "If we use medicine," they argue, "then we are not really trusting God." They do not disparage the work of doctors in the case of unbelievers, but feel that Christians, with real faith, should not need to resort to such "unspiritual" methods. (This view is expressed in Harold Horton's book, *The Gifts of the Spirit*, regarded by some pentecostals as a classic.)

I have always maintained that this anti-medical view is a distortion of Christian truth. This is shown by the fact that Jesus himself once said, "They that are whole have no need of a physician, but they that are sick . . ." (Mark 2:17 KJV).

Although He used these words in a spiritual connection,

they also show clearly that He didn't disparage the work of doctors. Indeed, had He done so, He would never have drawn the analogy between spiritual and physical health. On another occasion, Jesus commanded lepers He healed to "show themselves to the priests," the Jewish "doctors" who were able to certify their healing. In both these instances, Jesus was implicitly acknowledging the work of the doctors of His day, who were nothing like as knowledgeable or equipped as their modern counterparts.

We should also remember that oil and wine were the most common medicines of that time and that their use is not only approved, but even advocated in the Bible. (See Luke 10:34, Mark 6:13.) Paul urges Timothy, "Use a little wine for thy stomach's sake" (1 Tim. 5:23). Further biblical support for the ministry of medicine lies in the fact that Paul often had "Doctor" Luke with him on his journeys and that this companion is described as the "beloved" not the "out-of-work" or "ex" physician (Col. 4:14).

Once again, this time from the standpoint of the Bible, we see that there is no basic contradiction between divine healing and the world of medicine. God heals through both.

We must, however, go even further, and warn Christians who reject medical methods of healing that they are in danger of "putting God to the test." This sin was first committed by the Israelites as they journeyed from Egypt to the Promised Land. At one stage, they began to grumble about their lack of water and to make demands on God, which precipitated His supernatural intervention. This act, however, brought them under the judgment of God. (See Deuteronomy 6:16, Psalm 95:7-11, Hebrews 3:7-11, Exodus 17:7.)

Much later in the Bible story, Satan tried to entice Jesus into the same error when he argued that if Jesus jumped off the pinnacle of the Temple, He would be supernaturally protected and thereby prove that He was Messiah. Jesus knew that although this would be an "act of faith" on His part, yet He would be coercing His Father into unnecessary supernatural activity. He, therefore, replied, "It is written, you shall not tempt the Lord your God" (Matt. 4:7).

Certainly an Old Testament saint who did not fall into this trap was Nehemiah. When in danger from his foes, he commanded the people both to pray and *put sentries on duty* (Neh. 4:9). The provision of guards did not result from his "lack of faith." Nehemiah realized that he should take all the *normal* remedies at his hand and only then could he expect God to act supernaturally to protect His people, if the need arose.

Sick people who refuse good and necessary medical remedies which are at their disposal as "lack of faith" are *demanding* that God should act miraculously; indeed, they are trying to coerce Him into doing so. Although acting from the best motives, they have begun to "put God to the test." This can result in tragedy.

I can well remember a strained, bewildered, and desperate man coming to see me with a request that I should minister to his wife, who was at death's door with cancer. He explained that a year previously his wife had noticed a lump in her breast and, because they believed only in supernatural healing, they had decided not to consult their doctor.

"We wanted only the Lord to get the glory by a *real* miracle," he declared.

His wife's condition had, however, deteriorated rapidly, and now he looked for an even greater miracle at *my* hands.

"I now have a certainty God intends this miracle to be through *you*," he explained.

"If God is going especially to use *me*, I expect He will show *me*, as well as you, that this will be the case," I replied.

He was determined, on any account, not to consult his doctor.

In fact, I did not have to make a decision about it because a messenger came with the news that this lady had just died.

One cannot, of course, be dogmatic; maybe a mastectomy would not have prevented secondary growths. In any case, we know that this Christian woman is now in heaven. What this and similar cases *do* show, however, is that God will not necessarily act out of compulsion if we "put Him to the test."

My counsel therefore to sick people is that they should follow the advice of the Book of Ecclesiasticus* (Eccles. 38:1-14):

Honour a physician according to thy need of him, for verily the Lord hath created him. For from the Most High cometh healing—The Lord created medicines out of the earth and a prudent man will

---

* A book of the Apocrypha. The Apocrypha is accepted as canonical by the Roman Catholic Church, but is not in the Protestant Bible. This passage is always publicly read in the Church of England at St. Luke's tide.

have no disgust at them—with them He doth heal a man and taketh away his pain—My Son, in thy sickness, be not negligent. But pray unto the Lord and He shall heal thee. Put away wrongdoing, and order thine hands right and cleanse thy heart from all manner of sin—Then give place to the physician—there is a time when in their very hands is the issue for good.

Here is a perfect combination between divine healing and the world of medicine. A sick person should use medicine *and* divine healing ministry, trusting God to heal by either means, or both. He should *not* wait until the sickness is declared medically incurable before presenting himself for the laying on of hands. He should, from the beginning, avail himself of all the healing measures God has provided to reach him through spirit, mind, and body. He should follow his doctor's advice about medication, and regularly receive divine healing ministry, until he feels within himself that he is healed (Mark 5:29) and this has been confirmed by his doctor. Thanks can then be given to God for what is a definite and not a spurious healing.

Obviously such a view of supernatural healing today as cooperation between medicine and ministry narrows down the area left for "miracles." There will rarely be a "pure" one because doubters will always be able to say that because doctors were also treating the patient there is no *proof* that God intervened at all. This, however, should not distress us. Christians are not trying to prove the existence of God by the result of divine healing. Such a faith would rest on shaky foundations. Jesus himself constantly refused to pander to the contemporary demand for signs and wonders as grounds for believing in Him. (See Matthew 12:39, Mark 8:11, 13:22.) God will never trick people into belief and therefore always leaves the doubter a way of escape. Doctors and others today, who do not wish to believe, can always ultimately dart down the escape hatch of so-called "spontaneous remissions" if they want to avoid encounter with God. One doctor actually said to me: "I have no difficulty in believing your stories of healings, because I know that illnesses do remit in the most surprising ways. My difficulty is that so many do so immediately after you have laid hands on them!"

Perhaps he was not far from the kingdom of God!

Christians believe in God on other grounds than those of divine healing. They accept and experience the *whole* biblical panorama of God.

Divine healing, however, *does* add further evidence to encourage the faith of those *who wish* to believe. We see God's loving hand in the *total* healing process. Often definite indications of God's intervention are given through such events as a complete reversal in what doctors would normally have predicted to be the progress of a disease, the absence of expected pain or discomfort, instantaneous healing or *rapid* progress to health, results beyond those normally expected of usual medications, ability to dispense with sustaining drugs or appliances, disappearance of chronic deficiencies, and a new sense of the well-being of the whole person.

In this way, as for Jesus, the distinction between the natural and the supernatural rightly becomes blurred.

We also avoid a "God of the gaps" in human knowledge theology which has been destructive of faith in previous generations, as these gaps have, in fact, been filled. We are also "not guilty" of being totally irrational or bizarre. Healings are shown to be genuine and abound to the glory of God.

We acknowledge, however, that in the end, no matter how many times a person is healed, there will eventually be sickness which will cause him to die. Ministers, doctors, relatives, and friends will then have the satisfaction of knowing that they have done everything possible to heal, both from a spiritual and medical point of view. They can believe that the person has passed into a beautiful realm where our help is no longer necessary.

17

Life-Transforming Power

Death is an ever-present reality. It usually causes sorrow, and even the Bible, despite its message of everlasting life, acknowledges that the loss of loved ones will be accompanied by grief (1 Thess. 4:13-18). It was for this reason that Paul was so relieved when his friend Epaphroditus was spared from death that he did not have "sorrow upon sorrow" (Phil. 2:25-27).

It is inevitable, therefore, that some of those who ask for divine healing are seeking to postpone this somber event for themselves, their relatives and their friends. People usually become very desperate in the face of death. If, after ministry, the sick one does die, it can seem as if the ministry "hasn't worked," and that faithful prayer has not been answered. Wendy Jones challenged me about this on her "Midlands" television program. She made the matter very personal by asking a lady named Carol to appear before many thousands of viewers to represent the viewpoint of those for whom divine healing apparently had failed in its purpose.

Carol's was a particulary tragic case. She had been the

mother of two normal, healthy children, Paul and Michelle. Paul had been showing real promise at finishing school when he was suddenly stricken with a terminal brain disease. Hardly had Carol and her husband recovered from the shock when her daughter began to exhibit the same symptoms. It was eventually confirmed that she had the same terrible affliction. They were the only two cases of this rare illness known in England, and the situation was hopeless.

A long struggle began for these parents. Every possible medication was tried, but all to no avail. Carol had brought the children to church for ministry soon after receiving the news of their sickness and many hundreds of people believed with me for their healing. We repeatedly anointed the children with oil and used every other biblical method to reverse the seemingly inevitable progress of this deadly affliction. There were shouts of "Hallelujah" and "Praise the Lord" as we were once told that the march of the disease had been halted. Within weeks, however, our hopes were dashed as Paul became confined to a wheelchair. The battle went on as these parents still dared to believe for a miracle.

Michelle, the other child, had a terrible death. Her body jerked violently and uncontrollably as, covered with sweat, she slowly lost control of her faculties. Prayers were offered to the very end. Paul himself was continuing to deteriorate.

"Tell me," Wendy Jones challenged, "what help did these children receive?"

In reply, I expressed my deepest sympathy for the parents and praised their remarkable courage. Almost in tears, I was momentarily lost for words.

"They received every help," I replied quietly. "They received every help possible from the medical profession and we also did everything we could for them spiritually, this side of eternity."

It was then that Carol began to speak.

"I haven't come here to 'knock' Trevor," she said. "His ministry gave me hope when I had no hope. It was not a false hope, for I was hopeless. I would urge all mothers with incurable children to take them for ministry. It's benefits for me and my family have been beyond measure."

In fact, through this intense search for a miracle, Carol has found a deep and rich experience of God. She still comes to church to worship Him, whom, despite everything, she knows to be a loving heavenly Father. She has experienced the meaning, strength, love and courage of the cross.

She has also entered into the hope of the resurrection.

"Carol knows," I explained to the viewers, "that Michelle is in heaven." She treasures some verses which describe how God needs children as well as adults in His heavenly family.

Christian people seeking for an answer might well begin to accuse this lady of lack of faith, and search for other blockages in the healing process. One well-meaning Christian did tell Carol that it was her persistence in allowing the children to have drugs instead of trusting only God, which caused the bereavement. I have been more intent on praying for strength for these parents than entering into such a spiritual post-mortem.

In another such case there was again certainly no lack of faith. This was when Peter, a member of my own healing team, passed away at the age of fifty. Once again, this event was, from a spiritual point of view, shrouded in mystery.

Peter was ill for many months before doctors diagnosed that he had cancer in an advanced condition. They predicted that he would die within a few weeks. He was prescribed drugs, but given very little hope that they would even begin to be effective. We ministered healing to him and, almost immediately, he "miraculously" recovered. He actually returned to work and gave testimony in many places that God had wonderfully healed him. Peter was a man whose life was completely oriented on Jesus. He was absolutely wholehearted in his discipleship and service for his Lord.

He was, however, reprieved for only a year when suddenly he was stricken again with the dreadful disease. He and his wife confidently declared that God was going to heal him yet again. His last words to me were: "Trevor, the Lord is only allowing me to get so low so that there will be an even greater miracle for His glory. You watch! I'll be on my feet in a few days."

He eventually passed from this world to the next as angels surrounded him to take him to his heavenly home.

It has been my experience on such occasions that when relatives could have shown bitterness and resentment, gratitude, love, and hope have always prevailed. They have been given grace to submit to God's overruling and rested in the assurance that their loved one has entered into heavenly rest, health, and joy.

Life-Transforming Power

The secret of this transformation of attitudes lies, strangely enough, in the first miracle that Jesus ever performed—in Cana of Galilee (John 2). This first sign which He ever did was neither a healing, nor a raising of a man from the dead, but a turning of water into wine.

This was, in fact, an acted parable about *spiritual transformation*. Jesus transferred lifeless water into a powerful liquid, wine. This sets the scene for the rest of John's Gospel story, which is about the life-transforming power of Jesus over circumstances, sickness, and even death itself.

John is saying that when Jesus is admitted into a situation, whatever it may be, it is always transformed into a new richness, and given a new quality. So divine healing ministry brings Jesus into what would normally be tragic situations. Even when death occurs, He has, in fact, transformed death into the fullness of eternal life. (See John 11.)

"Failure" in divine healing occurs in our ministry because, unlike that of Jesus, it is *imperfect* (1 Cor. 13:9-12). We are not always able fully to convey God's healing power to those in need. This was even true of St. Paul. This man of faith and power had to write about his traveling companions that Epaphroditus was "sick nigh unto death," (Phil. 2:27 KJV) and "Trophimus I left ill at Miletus" (2 Tim. 4:20). There is even a possibility that Paul had an affliction himself which was never healed (2 Cor. 12:7-8).

If this giant of faith acknowledged his limitations, how much more should we! We are, for instance, often not as spiritually discerning as we should be about the deep causes of many of the sicknesses with which we are confronted. Neither are we always sure about the actual "area" in which we are ministering; whether, for instance, we are dealing with a case of "bruising" or one of demon possession. We are not always able to penetrate deeply enough to the guilt which lies at the root of some sicknesses in order to apply the word of forgiveness to the very point of need. Often we are not sensitive enough to the Spirit about the *method* we should use to bring healing, when to use a touch in the right place, or the right time to give a specific command. Ministers would also be very presumptuous if they claimed always to have that perfect faith which their Lord constantly exercised in His ministry. Likewise, although we do indeed have access to the supernatural healing gifts of discernment, faith, wisdom, knowledge, and prophecy, our use of them also frequently is imperfect. "Failure" in healing can often be related to the inadequacies of both the minister and the church. Paul says, "Now we see through a glass darkly" (1 Cor. 13:12 KJV). We must remember also that we live in a very rationalistic, unbelieving world, which constantly encroaches upon our spiritual life and saps our supernatural, life-transforming power.

Sick people themselves also often fall far short of the spiritual requirements which contribute to the reception of divine healing. Most, of course, are very sincere and many are even hopeful that some healing may take place. This, however, is far from even that faith which moves mountains of sickness.

I have sometimes stood in front of scores of sick people and realized, to my dismay, that many of them have come hoping for a "once for all" magic touch. This attitude was openly expressed by a woman I encountered in a television interview.

"I was sitting in a meeting and you made me wait for two hours before ministering to me, and I was in severe pain," she complained.

When I apologized and explained that at Power, Praise, and Healing meetings I always challenged people to commitment to Jesus before ministering to the sick, she made it obvious that she wanted nothing whatever to do with our wonderful Lord.

"I wrote you a letter of complaint," she retorted, "but did not give you my address, because I didn't want anyone coming 'round trying to convert me."

Obviously she wanted healing from Jesus, without commitment to Him. This, as we have seen, is not the way to experience the power which transforms sickness into health. No wonder she was not healed! There are many who, like her, go home disillusioned, thinking, "It hasn't worked: Christianity isn't true!" when all they have proved is that divine healing is not simply magical supernaturalism.

I have known many who have not been healed also because, basically, they have not *really* desired to be well. One such was a man who hobbled into a meeting on two crutches, obviously in intense pain. As I began to minister to him I realized that his crutches were, *for him*, more than a physical support; they were an emotional prop—a visible representation of his cry for help. I commanded him, in the name of the Lord, to let go of his wooden crutches and rest only on Jesus. The moment he did so he was healed. For several months he testified that Jesus had healed his back. However, the devil launched a counterattack upon him and, once again, he retreated into that sickness which subconsciously relieved him of many responsibilities and gained him sympathy. He grabbed his crutches and immediately his pain returned. Basically, the trouble was that he could not cope with the strain of being well.

I have known this *unconscious* holding on to a sickness also in many cases of neurosis, psychosis, addictions, and demon possession. The Lord will not transform people against their wills. Therefore, there must be a *complete* desire to be well on the part of those seeking help from His ministers.

In my experience, some failures in healing have resulted from sheer disobedience to Christ. This has sometimes been expressed in a refusal to respond to the healing word, sometimes in determination to carry on a life of dishonesty, or immorality, or a reluctance to live in the service of the Lord. In other cases, healing has not been forthcoming until barriers of resentment and bitterness towards God or others have been broken down, repented of, and forgiven. I well remember one case where a woman had to forgive her father's acts of rape and incest against her, and another where a person had to forgive her mother's cruelty to her, before their chronic depressions were transformed into peace and joy.

Some have not been healed because they have doubted that God really wanted to heal them. It is, in fact, best that seekers settle the matter of God's will in relation to their sickness before they come for healing. Jesus had to teach a leper this lesson when he came and said, "If you will, you *can* make me clean."

Being moved with compassion, Jesus replied, "I*will*; be clean" (Mark 1:40, italics mine).

I believe we can rest assured that Jesus' compassion is still extended to sick people in this way. They must, however, not only be sure that Jesus desires to heal them but also be certain that He is able to do so today, albeit through the ministry of His imperfect Church. Jesus once said, "All things are possible to him who believes" (Mark 9:23).

"Jesus Christ is the same yesterday and today and for ever" (Heb. 13:8). His willingness and His ability to achieve His desires *today* must, therefore, never be doubted, otherwise the ministry is robbed of power.

Despite all these hindrances to healing, we can keep on hoping, believing, trusting, and acting, confident that the life-transforming power of Jesus will still reach all those who truly seek Him. We have seen that His purposes can never ultimately be defeated, not even by death. He transforms everyone with whom He makes a real encounter. The testimony of the New Testament is that His perfect will is to make us and keep us whole, until it is time for Him to transform us into His own image in heaven. This is the burden of Paul's great prayer:

May the God of peace himself sanctify you wholly; and may your spirit and soul and body be kept sound and blameless at the coming of our Lord Jesus Christ. He who calls you is faithful, and he will do it. (1 Thess. 5:23-24)

We know from painful experience, however, that as yet, we do not see the answer to this and our Lord's own prayer, "Thy will be done on earth, as it is in heaven," but it is our task to see that despite our failures, it is realized as nearly as possible in our own time. That is why we minister and seek divine healing. When we do so, we are in the realm of the supernatural power of God. We are inviting Jesus into the sickness situation and can be confident that He will be present in His life-transforming glory. Wherever there is even the beginnings of a response, He *will* begin to act to bring His wholeness to spirit, soul, mind, and body. He is also always seeking to reveal and break down barriers to the healing process so that His purposes may be the more quickly realized.

Sometimes we instantaneously experience the results of His power in every area of our beings. Sometimes, however, the results are only gradually realized, for most healing is a process rather than an event. Always there must be an intense awareness of His presence and an expectancy of what He will do. There must, however, also be a deep submission of the life into His hands, acknowledging that He knows what is best for us all. When pain and suffering persists it must be brought to the cross itself, where Jesus will transform it to be a means of blessing and spiritual enrichment. Through divine healing ministry, sufferers will find grace to endure their sickness and witness through their courage, patience and even joy in their trials. The whole world has been enriched by the lessons learned through suffering and tragedy which has been surrendered to Jesus.

When we are ministering there will inevitably be

occasions when we will sense that the person is going to be healed through death. The person himself may realize that he is going to be transported to that sphere where he will have a resplendent, new, perfect body which will not suffer pain, decay, or death. (See 1 Corinthians 15:35-58, 2 Corinthians 5, Revelation 21:4.) This may be when the person has reached the allotted span of three score years and ten or when the Lord knows that their purpose on earth has been fulfilled. In these cases we know that he transforms death into life and tragedy into glory. Such is the transforming power of the presence of Jesus.

18

Supernatural
Healing Today

Thomas Hobbes, an English philosopher of the eighteenth century, once described human life as, ". . .nasty, brutish, and short." Thankfully, there have been many real changes for the better since his time. In the Western world at least, life is undoubtedly much easier and we have many pleasures to enjoy.

We owe a great deal of this progress to the achievements of science and technology. The advances made in the field of medical science alone have been truly remarkable. Therefore, most people can expect to live longer and be more free of infirmity, sickness, and pain than Hobbes could ever have imagined.

The successes of science, however, have led to a decline in religious belief and given birth to a new humanism as man has looked to his own skills, rather than to God, to solve his problems. In the West, because all forms of supernaturalism have been regarded either as side issues or a dangerous return to irrationalism, Christianity itself suffered a real eclipse. The most extreme attack on religion, however, was made by Karl Marx and the other classical communists whose thoughts have greatly influenced the anti-supernatural policy of many Eastern nations. Surprisingly, perhaps, many in the church have also deemed us to be living in a "post-Christian" society. Most people who have still dared to believe in God have, like myself, been taught that the Bible must be demythologized and our faith drastically reinterpreted, in order to make any sense in the modern world. Man's main problem now has seemed to be how best to distribute his new, self-acquired material blessings to the under-privileged nations and so avoid bloodshed, as he presses on to ever higher standards of living.

There are many indications, however, that the antisupernatural trend has been reversed, that mankind is not willing to be imprisoned in a purely physical, materialistic universe. He yearns to explore the supernatural dimension of life, which he is sure really exists. His heart is set upon a spiritual quest as well as upon a scientific one. Hence, there has recently been a world-wide comeback of the supernatural. Interest is intense. Satan has attempted to fill the spiritual vacuum by causing the phenomenal occult explosion of recent years: the spread of spiritualism, the resurgence of "black" and "white" magic, popular interest in astrology, and widespread involvement in transcendental meditation. The Holy Spirit has moved in with even more power in the supernatural revival called the charismatic movement. It is centered on a recovery of the supernatural gifts of tongues, interpretation of tongues, miracles, healing, discernment of spirits, wisdom, faith, knowledge, and prophecy. All this bears witness to the fundamental biblical truth that man has a spirit and a soul as well as a mind and body. His instincts cause him to desire rich spiritual experience. As St. Augustine said, "Thou hast made us for Thyself, and our hearts are restless, until they find their rest in Thee."

Christians know, however, that as there are both constructive and destructive material forces in the universe, so there are maleficent as well as beneficent spiritual powers. Our Lord Jesus said, "I saw Satan fall like lightning from heaven," (Luke 10:18) and He himself constantly came into conflict with the kingdom of evil.

St. Paul reiterated this truth: "We wrestle not against flesh and blood, but against principalities and powers . . . against spiritual wickedness in high places" (Eph. 6:12 KJV).

In the vast resurgence of supernaturalism today we have, therefore, a vital task, that of tuning people in to the right spiritual wavelength. We know that if human beings sell their souls to the devil, disaster, worse than any invasion from outer space, will inevitably follow. We Christians are not simply supernaturalists, we are po'nting mankind to a faith that is true, healthy, rational, and good and which can bring incalculable benefits to mankind.

Another factor of immense importance in the world today is that the complications and pressures involved in living in our modern society have produced what can almost be described as a plague of neuroses and psychoses. Psychiatrists and sociologists seem to be nowhere near controlling this epidemic which threatens to become beyond control. Tranquilizers and sedatives are prescribed in ever-increasing, gigantic proportions as marriages increasingly collapse and the suicide rate rises ever higher. All over the world people are crying out for help and turning beyond man, to God, in order to find it. This is one of the prime causes of the renewed interest in supernatural healing today.

Another is that, as our physical sense of well-being has increased through the advances of medicine, so also we have become far more sensitive to those pains and ills which Hobbes and his contemporaries took for granted as part of our lot. People have always lived under the sentence of death but now we feel that *we have a right* to a full and happy life until we are at least seventy years of age. Medical science, which has increased our average life expectancy, has proved far from able to answer all the needs to which it has drawn attention.

Once again, therefore, people are turning to God to see if He can or will help the children whom He has created overcome their physical and mental sicknesses.

Supernatural healing is increasingly a fact of our time and, unless I am very much mistaken, it is here to stay. Christians, however, have precisely the same task in this realm as they have in that of more general religious experience. We must show our fellows that there are both true and false methods of spiritual healing, and point to the sphere of divine healing as that which truly emanates from God.

A great responsibility for *teaching* now lies at the door of the Church, which bases its ministry on that of Jesus Christ—the most wonderful, effective, and pure healing ministry ever known in history. It is our duty to point out that divine healing is concerned with the welfare of the *whole* person, body, mind, and spirit, and that this flows from a deep, personal relationship with God. As Christians, we have knowledge of a God who is so much aware of human pain and suffering that He has entered into the very midst of it in order to experience, bear, and redeem it. Our God hangs in agony on a cross. We are able also to proclaim to all mankind the real possibility of entering into a deep personal relationship with God on the basis of the forgiveness of our sins through the self-sacrifice of His Son, Jesus Christ. "God was in Christ, reconciling the world unto himself . . ." (2 Cor. 5:19).

The Christian message is that God has not left mankind without hope, but that He is still able to be found by those who seek Him, for He dwells in and with His people. We declare that the Church, despite all its weaknesses and failures, has been called into being by God's activity, and that it has been commissioned and supernaturally endowed for a ministry of divine healing. We have seen, in fact, that, as it looks to its Lord in awareness, expectation, obedience, and love, it *can* communicate His healing power to bruised, broken-hearted, possessed, sick, and spiritually destitute people. The Church is therefore not so much an *institution* as a *people*, supernaturally anointed to extend the ministry of Jesus to every age.

We have seen that the people of God have not only been given a commission to fulfill, but also *ways* by which to channel supernatural healing to their fellows. They minister the power of His Spirit through the use of dedicated hands, words, oil, and other faith-aids in the ways they have seen successfully practiced by their Lord.

In the midst of so much that is bogus, bizarre, and counterfeit they explain that divine healing is not magical but depends on relationships. Basically, it is an abiding communion with God through Jesus of history, who is still very much alive today.

Christians preach that God created the human race and then redeemed it and that, therefore, He is the Lord God of the natural order and the supernatural. His Spirit is to some extent at work in the hearts of all men of good will. For this reason believers are able to accept and use all the healing resources in the natural world and fully cooperate with medical science. Nevertheless, the results of Christian ministry can never be limited to those obtained by the methods of medical science; they are not fully predictable but stretch beyond anything human beings can either imagine or conceive. Divine healing ministry is not irrational and its exponents are not cranks; on the contrary, we have a wisdom which comes from God, because we love God and our fellow-men with our minds as well as with our hearts. Once the existence of God and the spiritual-psychosomatic nature of man are accepted, divine healing is both reasonable and credible.

Despite our war on sickness and infirmity, we Christians are not afraid of pain. We are not looking for a soft, comfortable cotton-wool existence. We have been challenged by a crucified Lord to take up our own cross and follow Him (Matt. 16:21-28). We realize that pearls of incalculable price have been wrought in the treasure chest of tragedy, because it was so with the cross itself. We know that God is able to redeem the deepest evils, sufferings, and pains, and make them work together for good (Rom. 8:28). We know also that, like our Lord, we have been called to a mission of tears and toil, misunderstanding, rejection, and persecution. Yet we cannot shrink back from self-denying, self-sacrificing love for others. (See 1 Peter 1:6-7, 1 Peter 2:18-25.)

The Christian healing mission is, therefore, both evangelistic and pastoral. We must go out beyond the confines of our own charismatic communities, to proclaim the good news of God's healing, sustaining love to those who either do not know it, or who have misunderstood and, therefore, rejected it. Our duty is to call men and women to respond to God's initiative by an act of faith, love, and obedience. Once this response has been made, pastoral divine healing can begin, within the pastoral domain of the church.

Divine healing is, in fact, best seen in its pastoral context, because at its deepest it is more of a lifelong *process* than a miraculous *event*. It involves the body-life of the church, as Christians minister to one another, through their appointed leadership. We know that in this fallen world everyone will have a lifelong struggle—against sickness of the body, anxiety of mind, assaults of the devil, and sin in the soul. It is by divine healing ministry, within the community of believers, that life's wounds can constantly be bathed in God's grace. From that community also, prayers of faith can wing their way to heaven as we believe in God for the healing of individuals, societies, nations, and even the world.

Christians are committed to belief in the life-transforming power of the presence of Jesus.

Therefore, while we are very realistic about the sin and sickness which corrupt and destroy the human race, we remain intense optimists. We know that with God there is no situation which is beyond redemption. We can look even death, decay, and disaster in the face, and know that Jesus can transform them into life and blessing. Our Lord has himself risen from the dead, and, therefore, we can experience that we are "more than conquerors through him who loved us" (Rom. 8:37).

We sing with Charles Wesley:

Finish then Thy new creation
Pure and spotless let us be,
Let us see Thy great salvation
Perfectly restored in Thee.
Changed from glory into glory
Till in heaven we take our place,
Till we cast our crowns before Thee,
Lost in wonder, love and praise.

and

He bids us build each other up
Till gathered into one
To our high calling's glorious hope
We, hand-in-hand, go on.

For free information on how to receive
the international magazine

LOGOS JOURNAL

also Book Catalog

Write: Information - LOGOS JOURNAL CATALOG
Box 191
Plainfield, NJ 07061